5 75

SO-BBD-647

A LETTER TO A YOUNG PAINTER

# A LETTER
# TO A
# YOUNG PAINTER

Herbert Read

HORIZON PRESS · NEW YORK

First American Edition 1962
Library of Congress Catalog Card No. 62-17009

© 1962 Trustees of the Discretionary Trust
MARGARET READ, AMBROSE APPELBE AND WILLIAM READ
PRINTED IN GREAT BRITAIN BY THE CAMELOT PRESS

# CONTENTS

# LIST OF PLATES

Part I

A LETTER TO A YOUNG PAINTER

# A LETTER TO A YOUNG PAINTER

I PROMISED, on returning from Venice, to describe more clearly (and at greater length!) the impressions that your paintings had made on me in the course of the two or three visits I paid to your studio. Those visits were memorable – memorable in the sense that I carried away with me distinct images of your work. So often, after a private view, one is left with a general impression which may indeed be pleasurable, and perhaps pleasurable just because it remains diffuse. But in your case the images were so aggressive that they remained in my mind in all their original clarity. This is not necessarily a point in their favour – there are visual experiences that haunt us like nightmares, and one would gladly be rid of them. The images you paint have this haunting quality, and the first question I ask myself is whether this has any bearing on their aesthetic merits. Might they not remain as acute memory images precisely because they have some penetrating psychotic quality? I don't mean a quality that is necessarily morbid – as you know, I have been much attracted to the psychology of Jung and I think of these images as *archetypal*, as he would say, and what is archetypal is anything but morbid: the archetype is rather the

symbol of completeness, of integrity, of the individual's rest in Abraham's bosom. But the artist
must wander about and about before he can reach
this point of rest.

If we look at the work of the Italian painters in
the Biennale this year – Afro, Birolli, Corpora,
Moreni, Morlotti, Santomaso, Turcato, Vedova
(I rattle off their names because I have a book of
illustrations which Santomaso gave me the evening
I met you), one can always see, either that they are
playing with a naturalistic motive, elaborating and
distorting it until they get an abstract pattern
which satisfies their aesthetic sensibility; or, like
Vedova, they take an abstract theme ('Aspirazione',
'Sbarramento', etc.) and evolve a design which is a
symbol for the idea. In your case, if I am not
mistaken, the idea is never abstract, never conceptual. You may have a motive (the conductor,
which conveys certain abstract qualities such as
dynamism, psychic energy, musical harmony),
but it is derived neither from nature nor from
calculation. It is an autonomous image – the bull,
the horse, the owl, etc. – and this image is an
archetype, not personal to you, but universal,
primordial, and you give it a form and colours
which again are not personal, not aesthetic, but
communicated to you from the unconscious,
directly. It is enormously vital (the result), but
it is not art. Nor is it *décor*. It is potentially something much greater than Afro, Birolli, Corpora,

etc. (let us call them A.B.C.), and yet it lacks an element which, for all their inadequacy, makes A.B.C. genuine artists. We joked about 'sensations', and about the importance of 'realizing' one's sensations. If you read the letters of Van Gogh and Cézanne, you will see what supreme importance they attached to this process of 'realization', this translation of sensation into the *matière* of painting. Every 'point' of the painting has to have this realized quality, this sense that it has been felt, that it is the equivalent of a sensation. If you can combine this quality with the psychic energy you already so abundantly (and so strangely) possess – ah, then!

But how? I can't tell you. It can only be told in paint. I can only say 'yes' or 'no' to your attempts. I will only say this: that when I looked up, that first Sunday morning, and saw the canvas which you had transformed in a few minutes, I felt speechless. A mystery had been revealed to me – what Lawrence called 'the most superb mystery we have hardly recognized – the immediate instant self . . . the quick of all the universe, of all creation. . . .' Lawrence's language is too vague, too emotional, and we still lack an adequate philosophy of art. What is 'realized' in an act of creation is certainly something more than (greater in significance than) the self. The self (that is to say, an individual state of consciousness) is capable of apprehending something beyond the self. The consciousness, at the moment of creation, is in a state of readiness, alertness, awareness, and is then capable of extension or *dilation*; but at the same time, of co-ordination.

One of the few people who have written any sense about art was Conrad Fiedler – the friend of Hans vonMarées and Hildebrand. He wrote in the '70's and '80's, but he has not been superseded by all our modern psychology of art. The following extract from his neglected writings is to me an amazing anticipation of the aesthetic foundations of modern painting and of special relevance to your own creative effort:

'It is a chief requirement of artistic talent that it shall possess an especially refined and sensitive susceptibility to certain qualities of things. In pre-eminent artists we may, indeed, occasionally meet with that profound relationship of sensation and of a feeling for the totality of natural objects. But the presence of such refined feelings is not yet an indication of artistic talent. To possess such feelings is the main prerequisite for artistic as well as for every other mental productiveness; for he who does not seek to grasp nature with the power of his intuition will never succeed in subjugating her to his higher mental consciousness. *But the artist becomes an artist by virtue of his ability to rise above his sensations.* It is true that sensation accompanies him in all the phases of his artistic activity and keeps him continuously in a close relationship to all things, that it nourishes in him the warmth of life by which he himself is connected with the world. *Sensation continuously provides him with the material the transformation of which is the fulfilment of his mental existence.* Yet, however heightened his sensations may be, he must always be able to master them with the clarity of his mind. And although the artist's creation is possible only on the basis of an extraordinarily intense feeling, nevertheless this artistic creation has been made possible by his still more extraordinary power of mind, which even in moments of the most intense sensory experience preserves unimpaired the calmness of objective interest and the energy of formative creation.'*

Fiedler is afraid that the mind will not master the sensory experience, but your danger is the opposite one – that sensation does *not* accompany you in all the phases of your painterly activity and keep you continuously in a close relation to all things. This is not a question (as Fielder might have thought) of retaining a naturalistic element in your painting; but simply that your painting does not always remain true to perceptual experience. The mind (particularly the impersonal, unconscious aspect of your mind) throws a mask of symbolism over your sensations. You do not merely rise above

* *On Judging Works of Visual Art.* Trans. by Henry Schaefer-Simmern and Fulmer Wood. University of California Press, 1957, pp. 30-31.

your sensations – you lose all contact with them.

More Fiedler: 'Artistic achievements always spring anew from a domain which must remain inaccessible to the influence of intellectualizing reflection. . . .

'Art does not start from abstract thought in order to arrive at forms; rather, it climbs up from the formless to the formed, and in this process is found its entire mental meaning.'

There you have the justification (or, at least, the explication) for that method in modern painting (Masson, Jackson Pollock, Riopelle, Appel, Saura, de Kooning, Joan Mitchell, you yourself) which is not, as so often assumed, spontaneous calligraphy (for which another kind of aesthetic justification is necessary – one that was formulated centuries ago by the Chinese), but rather the kind of art described by Fiedler. In your kind of painting, as I see it, there is this process, this 'climbing up from the formless'; and the interest, and the excitement of it, comes from the discoveries made on the way.

I think I must burden you with another quotation, this time from a contemporary philosopher, Karl Jaspers: 'We must distinguish', he has written, 'between art as an expression of a particular aesthetic ideal and art as a code of symbols for metaphysical reality. The two coincide only when beauty happens to reveal transcendent reality, when such reality is experienced as beautiful, and when everything is seen as essentially beautiful for the reason that it is real. The term "great art" we reserve for metaphysical art – that is to say, an art whose visible creations reveal the underlying reality. It is axiomatic that all representation not so self-transcendent – all mere decoration, all performance which merely charms the senses – can never be more than art in the sense of technical cleverness with no relation to philosophy. This holds true wherever the aesthetic has become divorced from metaphysical contexts.'*

The extraordinary thing is, that this distinction solemnly made by a solemn philosopher, you and other artists of your kind have already discovered. Your art aims to be 'a code of symbols for metaphysical reality' but Jaspers might say that it does not (yet) express 'a particular aesthetic ideal' because you do not experience transcendent reality as beautiful. I differ from Jaspers in that I would reserve the term 'great art' for a unity of the beautiful and the vital, of the metaphysical and the physical, of the mathematical and the organic. Jaspers does not give any illustrations of what he means by 'metaphysical art'. He would probably, if pressed, mention Michelangelo! But Michelangelo would be just as good an illustration for my point of view, for in his case transcendent truth is never divorced

* *Tragedy is not Enough.* Trans. H. A. T. Reiche, H. T. Moore, K. W. Deutsch. Boston (U.S.A.) 1952; London 1953, p. 26.

17

from sensuous corporeality (the spirit made flesh).

It is my turn to be solemn, but the same strife of opposites is present in Cézanne, in Picasso – artists who are not so obviously 'metaphysical' as Michelangelo. The whole point is: metaphysical statements can be made in visual terms. Jaspers is right: five apples on a plate can be a statement of transcendental truth.

My emphasis (and Fiedler's) is on form – the form that must be wrested from chaos; but this does not mean that we can neglect the question of colour.

I once persuaded a teacher to let her children paint 'unconscious' pictures, 'mind pictures' as they were called. The children were told to stop thinking (a difficult discipline for children!), to close their eyes and sit very still, and then to paint the pictures that came into their minds. The results were remarkable – mostly like early Kandinsky's, 'organic abstractions', with a strong tendency towards those patterns which the Jungian psychologists call 'mandalas' (the teacher herself was not a psychologist). But another interesting circumstance was that the colour schemes were quite different from those which the children used for their normal painting. They were consistent for each child, not at all pretty, but violent and sometimes gloomy.

I became convinced on the basis of that one experience that colours have an unconscious symbolic value – perhaps a different value for each person, perhaps a value for each 'complex'. I immediately felt, when I saw your paintings, that your colours were symbolic in this sense.

Colour is, of course, always closely related to personality, even when the choice is conscious. The colours of El Greco, Rubens, Tintoretto, Delacroix, Renoir, Cézanne, Matisse, Picasso – how instinctively we know that they reveal the essential character of each of these artists. To that extent they are not controlled by a conscious aesthetic. But there are degrees of nearness to the unconscious. How near El Greco is, and how far away Renoir, or Matisse! And Picasso? He began in the same aesthetic of colour harmony as Renoir or Toulouse-Lautrec. But in his cubist period he suddenly becomes grey and sombre, almost colourless. Then he slowly returns to colour, and by 1920 his colour is liberated again, full of gaiety. He now has such control of his means of expression that he can be gay or sombre at will, but he is least gay when he is most symbolic, as in *Guernica*. *Guernica* is a collection of unconscious symbols (how much Picasso knew about their psychological significance is doubtful) and they have no colour. (Some people say there is no colour in their dreams.)

*Guernica* is no doubt metaphysical art, in Jaspers' sense of the term. I don't think Jaspers would be satisfied to call *Still Life with Mandolin and Guitar* (1924) an example of metaphysical art, of 'great art'. Alas, it merely 'charms the senses'. But the greatness of Picasso is just in this fact: that he has abolished the distinction made by Jaspers. I cannot honestly say that *Guernica* is a 'greater' painting than the *Still Life*. I know that if it came to a choice of which picture to live with, I would choose the *Still Life*—but that is no criterion—I would not like to live with a Michelangelo! Greatness is not an attribute of works of art—only the artist is great, and a great artist must sometimes play, must reveal all aspects of his personality, and above all *must not lock himself up in the cage of the unconscious*. He must not be afraid of freedom, even freedom from the promptings of his unconscious.

Your painting is nevertheless an attempt to penetrate direct to the abyss, to the unconscious. It is much more disturbing, in the sense that it is an expression of the will to dominate. (Love, said Goethe, does not dominate, it cultivates—and that is more.) I am almost on the point of telling you that there is no love in your painting, and yet you have said that it is a kind of love-making. But the love is consumed in the 'making'; your colour and *facture* is burnt up, and only dark ashes are left. Painting—true painting—is a different kind of love: what Saint Ailred called 'the palate of the heart' which finds all creation sweet. You must love painting, but to try to dominate the motif, with an obsessive fury, merely leads to sensuous exhaustion, to sterility.

The Chinese are instinctively right about

everything connected with the process of painting a picture or writing a poem. There are many writings by the painters themselves, but for the moment I can think only of a passage in the *Tao-tê-ching* which says something profound about the right moment of stopping:

> Stretch a bow to the very full,
> And you will wish you had stopped in time;
> Temper a sword-edge to its very sharpest,
> And you find it soon grows dull. . . .
> When your work is done, then withdraw!
> Such is Heaven's way.

A work of art is like a fruit that matures, and when it is ripe it just drops off. But it must drop off in calm weather, in a state of serenity. If it is tossed off in a storm it will be bruised.

You tell me that you want to paint 'states of mind', tired people, people with *Sehnsucht*, etc., and you ask me if that is a wrong point of departure. It is, I think, an unusual one – it shows that you are fundamentally an expressionist (as are nearly all Jewish artists). Expressionism is as legitimate as any other type of art, if the result *is* art (as it is in Soutine for example). I have often asked myself why is it that most French and English people do not like expressionist art, and I have never found a satisfactory answer. It is perhaps because it reveals too much; perhaps because it has no serenity, and life is so full of conflict and *malheur* that we seek

*Erlösung* in art. I think that was always the main function of art – certainly of Greek art and Christian art (think of the madonnas at Torcello and Murano). I think that fundamentally I too always seek *Erlösung* in art, and I don't find it in Nolde and Kirchner and Kokoschka and all their kind. Nor, of course, in A.B.C.

But I haven't answered your question. In a certain sense I do not think it matters where the painter starts from (and I think Picasso once said something of the kind); what matters is where he arrives at, and that, you see, must be a closed form, an objective 'thing of beauty' that is a 'joy for ever'. I don't mean beauty in any conventional academic sense – Soutine is beautiful in the sense I mean. Take, for example, that *Pollo appeso al chiodo* at the Biennale (No. 29) or even the *Bue squartato* – how the colours sing and vibrate and entrance one. And how well he paints a state of mind (the *Ritratto di ragazzo in blu*, for example) without any sacrifice of sensuous colour.

I can understand your suppression of colour – you are painting 'mind' pictures, and the colours are compulsive. But to the percipient outsider it is almost as if you were afraid of being 'pretty' or 'sentimental'. One must not divorce colour from form in this way. It is almost as if you said to yourself: Form is self-sufficient – I won't dilute it with colour. Yes – it can be self-sufficient, and you quite rightly point to Marcel Duchamp and certain phases of Picasso (but what minor phases they are in Picasso's whole career, how they are obliterated by his more radiant works!). I think Duchamp is a bad example to follow – remember that for all his intelligence (too much) and for all his importance at the beginning of the modern movement, he is an artist *raté*, and it may be that he became *raté* because he realized that he had no sensibility for colour. That you have sensibility you have proved by a sketch I saw in Venice. But for some reason, no doubt a deep and serious reason, you are inhibiting your joy in colour.

You are perfectly right to object to that phrase I used about 'living with a picture'. Perhaps I have been influenced too much by Matisse's extraordinary statement – do you remember it?:

'What I dream of is an art of balance, of purity and serenity devoid of troubling or depressing subject-matter, an art which might be for every mental worker, be he businessman or writer, like an appeasing influence, like a mental soother, something like a good armchair in which to rest from physical fatigue.'

As an expression of bourgeois banality that, I imagine, infuriates you as it would have infuriated Tolstoy! I do not think it should be divorced from many other statements which Matisse has made about art; and it was written in 1908, in a world free from *Angst*! But still, it does express a certain truth – I mean, an historical truth. That is what art has been at many periods, for most people. 'An art of balance, purity and serenity'—doesn't that describe Giotto, and Piero della Francesca, Seurat and Cézanne? But *not*, you will protest, all artists —not Rembrandt or El Greco, Picasso or Henry Moore. Instead of balance they have chaos, instead of purity they have passion, and instead of serenity they have anxiety. Instead of *beauty* they have *vitality*, and *that*, you will say, is something 'greater' than beauty.

But no, not greater. The *one* thing that *all* art must aim for is a certain enhancement of the process of being, the affirmation of life, and of the significance of human destiny. Without that, there is only nihilism, or various forms of self-deception. That *Bejahung*, enhancement, can be achieved in at least two ways (perhaps fundamentally only two). One is a *Bejahung* on the surface of life, accepting the sensuous thrill of colours, the harmony of forms, all that is vivid and expressive in nature; the other is an inward *Bejahung*, an acceptance of the promptings of instinct, the upsurging pressures of an expanding personality, the discoveries of consciousness (of meditation and inward attention), and above all the impersonal intimations of the unconscious (and these are the archetypes, the forms which come unbidden, but imperious, demanding expression).

One cannot associate either purity or serenity with this second type of art. Not even in the case of Cézanne. 'What forces our interest is Cézanne's anxiety – that's Cézanne's lesson; the torments of van Gogh – that is the actual drama of the man. The rest is sham.' (Picasso said that.) But even so, there is *Erlösung* (one must use this German word because an English word like 'deliverance' does not express the whole experience). Cézanne or van Gogh might never succeed, to their own satisfaction, but what they were striving for was an *Erlösung*. It is only if we can achieve *Erlösung* that we can continue to live, or to feel alive.

Yes: pictures are not things to be lived with, on comfortable terms. Fundamentally, they are things to be painted as an expression of inner life, and we, the spectators, ought to be interested in the inner life of the artist, and not in so many square-inches of décor for our sitting-rooms. But again listen to Picasso:

'How can you expect an onlooker to live a picture of mine as I have lived? A picture comes to me from miles away: who is to say from how far away I sensed it, saw it, painted it; and yet the next day I can't see what I've done myself. How can anyone enter into my dreams, my instincts, my desires, my thoughts, which have taken a long time to mature and to come out into the daylight, and above all grasp from them what I have been about – perhaps against my own will?'

'It's not what the artist *does* that counts, but what he *is*'. Yes: but he must tell us what he is, in language (visual symbols) which we can understand,

and no one knows better than Picasso how to make that language expressive – expressive of the man he is. He can't tell us how he does it – 'I deal with painting as I deal with things, I paint a window just as I look out of a window. If an open window looks wrong in a picture, I draw a curtain and shut it, just as I would in my own room. In painting, as in life, you must act directly.'*

He works in the same way with colours. 'At the actual time that I am painting a picture I may think of white and put down white. But I can't go on working all the time thinking of white and painting it. Colours, like features, follow the changes of the emotions. You've seen the sketch I did for a picture with all the colours indicated on it. What is left of them? Certainly the white I thought of, and the green I thought of, are there in the picture, but not in the places I intended, nor in the same quantities. Of course, you can paint pictures by matching up different parts of them so that they go quite nicely together, but *they'll lack any kind of drama.*'

Forgive me if I am repeating statements by Picasso which are familiar to you, but they seem to be so relevant to your own problem.

With extraordinary perception you seem to have gone straight to the heart of the matter, as

* These quotations are taken from a statement made by Picasso in 1935, translated and reproduced in *Picasso: Fifty Years of his Art*. By Alfred H. Barr, Jr. New York (Museum of Modern Art), 1946.

revealed by Picasso. That is to say, you do not want to 'paint pictures by matching up different parts of them so that they go quite nicely together' – you want to give them some kind of drama.

I also begin to see how you propose to work in this further statement of Picasso:

'When you begin a picture, you often make some pretty discoveries. You must be on your guard against these. Destroy the thing, do it over several times. In each destroying of a beautiful discovery, the artist does not really suppress it, but rather transforms it, condenses it, makes it more substantial. What comes out in the end is the result of discarded finds. Otherwise, you become your own connoisseur. I sell myself nothing.'

How wonderful that is – *I sell myself nothing!* But the difficulty, as I have said before, is to know when to stop – the psychological moment, as they say. Picasso gives no clue to this – in fact, he does not know – there is no rule. He says 'When I begin a picture, there is somebody who works with me. Towards the end, I get the impression that I have been working alone – without a collaborator.' That is it – you stop when you feel alone with your picture, perhaps identical with it. I know the same feeling in writing a poem: either there are two forces at work, the critical self and the emotional self, and they try to agree; or (and this is when the poem is 'right') there is just one Self, and the Self *is* a poem, and the poem is the Self.

One more word about colour. Picasso: 'Actually, you work with few colours. But they seem like a lot when each one is in the right place.' That is the point. Those early cubist paintings never seem dull or colourless – on the contrary, they are *rich*. But *rich*! You may say – what about my blacks and greens and indigos? Well, there is nothing wrong with such colours in themselves, but they are dramatic – sooty, fuliginous, tragic – and that is perhaps my objection to them. They are too directly symbolic. In a Picasso there may be very few colours – some greys and browns, or (*Les Demoiselles d'Avignon*) browns, rose pink, blue, grey – but the drama is in the colours, their *acôtement*, as you would say, just in that, and not in their symbolism, not in what each separately conveys emotionally. Picasso says 'drama'; I say *Spielerei* – it is the same thing, for a drama must be *played*. *Spielerei* is not necessarily trivial, *kitschig*, etc. It may be a 'play of the imagination', where the word *play* has two senses, *Spiel* and Drama (Eros and Agon). Schiller understood this, so did Nietzsche, who gave me my favourite maxim: everything divine runs on light feet. The artist's progress is a dance with colours, kaleidoscopic; between one painting and another the change may be infinitesimal, invisible. But gradually the artist reveals himself, his vital sensibility.

Sometime I would like to see some of your rough sketches, pencil drawings, naturalistic notes, anything that is unpremeditated and spontaneous – a 'thumb-nail sketch', such as you might scribble in a letter, something less finished than the gouache you gave me, and something more objective. It would be a little confession, and I would not be so silly as to criticize it. But it might tell me something – think how much Rembrandt's sketches tell us that we would never know if we had seen only the finished oils.

I have laid this letter aside because I have been absorbed all week in the sculpture lectures for Washington, and have just written the last sentence of the last of them.

What is the conclusion of it all? That sculpture is the greatest of the plastic arts, certainly. That Michelangelo, Rodin and Moore are the greatest sculptors, probably. But that there is no art in which such *confusion* has reigned – confusion of aim, confusion of technique, confused appreciation. I feel as though I had been cleaning out a cellar or lumber-room – but what does one do with so much rubbish?

There are features of your own work which suggest to me that you should be a sculptor rather than a painter. Perhaps when you get to Paris you might try working a little in clay or wax, almost secretly, just for yourself and for me. You must not, until you feel sure of yourself in this medium, break the development of your painting, which is now proceeding so quickly. But your painted forms are really sculptural in conception – they are not paintings *in* two dimensions, but paintings *of* three-dimensional forms, and you always, it seems to me, have difficulty in relating your forms to the rectangle of the picture-frame. And the reason why you work so slowly – this 'choosing all the time' – is because your form does not grow on the canvas, like an image coming into focus, but grows in your mind, and you have to be sure, in your mind, of the precise outline of the image before you begin to paint it. Maybe that is one way of painting (Blake's way, the Gothic way) but in painterly painting colour *spreads*; form *thickens* (cf. the German word for poetry: *Dichtung*).

Do not think of shells and carcasses – these are dead discarded forms. Think rather of the mould or matrix, of the womb-like forms predetermined for the living being. Think always in terms of life, of germination; never in terms of death, of petrifaction. There is in the Germanic-Jewish soul an unconscious death wish – German poetry is full of it, and it dominates German philosophy to-day (Heidegger, for example, and a psychologist like Freud). It is the source of all nihilism and despair. It is the sin against the Holy Ghost, to which the early Christians succumbed. For the Holy Ghost, in the only sense in which I can believe in it, is the spirit of wonder and echantment, Simone Weil's 'grace' (her 'gravity' is another name for the death wish).

The world, particularly our world of artists and poets, is a desperate world of strife and envy, of ambition and despair, of intrigue and insincerity, and it is not only the good who survive. One has to be terribly strong-minded and patient, humble and unworldly. And the greatest danger is success! All this you know, and if it were only a question of art, and of your struggle as an artist, you would not despair. Your despair comes from other causes: from your frustrated emotions and from your family tension. This, too, you know. But you sometimes confuse your subjective *malheur* with your creative struggles; and if the work does not succeed, you associate your personal unhappiness with this practical failure. Of course, when the work goes well, then you get so much happiness from it that you forget your personal misery. And that is what must be made to happen all the time – from strength to strength in your work, with no time or heart-space for *Weltschmerz*. The only joy is in creation, and *Weltschmerz* in general is due to the fact that most people in our modern civilization have no 'joy-in-creation' – they are alienated, slaves to machines, robots in a waste land.

Don't get too fussed about the sculptural problem. I think this is the dilemma: either you have a *Gestalt* which exists in and for itself, and is best represented in three-dimensional plasticity; or you have a rectangle of canvas which you must fill with an all-over design. If you merely project on to the canvas a representation of a three-dimensional *Gestalt*, then you ignore the two-dimensional frame of reference which is the canvas (either ignore, or fill in with meaningless, functionless areas of paint).

The forms on a canvas can either fly off into space, or come in from space towards a centre, or simply satisfactorily fill the rectangle. But they must be related to the limits of the canvas – in a Poussin, a Cézanne, a Klee, a Picasso, we are not conscious of the frame because the composition coheres within it (and without it). Even those simple severe portraits of the Renaissance are always like heads that look out of a window: the space round them is intimately linked to the central mass. In Rembrandt the painting of the space behind a head is as important as the painting of the head itself: it is all one space conception.

Perhaps I can illustrate what I mean:

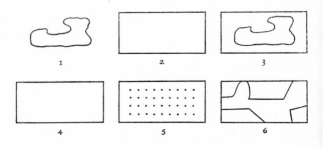

This is elementary and obvious, but *1, 2* and *3* illustrate what I mean by a sculptural painting – first the form, then the frame, and then the frame round the form. *4, 5* and *6* illustrate the painterly painting – first the frame, then the space within the frame and then the form filling the space within the frame. Of course, it would never be the same form – a form conceived from the beginning as three-dimensional (*1*) is one kind of form; a form conceived as occupying a two-dimensional area (*6*) would be quite a different form. And I have ignored the function of colour, which helps to knit together the divisions which the forms make within the frame.

As you know, works of art have been submitted to geometrical analysis and there is now a whole science of 'dynamic symmetry'. Much of it is unnecessary and boring, but one general law, applicable to all works of art whatsoever, seems to have emerged. It is this:

'We have found, in considering the most remarkable productions of all periods, that in each of these one fundamental shape is repeated, so that the parts by their adjustment and disposition reproduce similar figures. Harmony results only from the repetition of the principal figure throughout the sub-divisions of the whole' (Thiersch).

That means, in relation to a canvas, that the space is so sub-divided that any part has a harmonious relationship to the other parts and to the whole.

33

There are no gaps not covered by this harmonious 'lattice' (*graticcio*).

But, of course, the artist does not generally arrive at this result by geometrical calculation: it is the instinctive law of composition.

Of one thing I feel sure – you should work out your formal elements more clearly, as Kandinsky always did, before you combine them on the canvas. This may seem to contradict what I have said about the need for spontaneity, but not really. I mean that one must instinctively command the calligraphic strokes, as the Chinese painter does as a result of his exercises. All this painting and repainting of the same canvas – that is surely wrong. It not only means 'tired' paint (messy *matière*), but also exhaustion. I know, of course, that one must modify as one goes along, and that an idea in ink or crayon on paper becomes another idea when it is painted in oils on canvas. But you should be able to allow (mentally) for that degree of transformation. First perfect your alphabet of signs – that has been the practice of all great artists, though of course some write more clearly and more quickly than others.

You say you have clear ideas in the beginning but that they become obscure as you go along. But those ideas are only clear in your imagination. If they were first in the form of clear images, they could not become obscure when transferred to canvas.

The shock of pleasure one gets from a painting is the shock of a revived experience, of a communicated sensation. One must *feel* the sensation, along the nerves, in the brain. Didn't Cézanne talk about his 'petite *sensation*'? *Sensation, révélation* (Braque).

Sensation of what? *Crin contre crin*\* – partly visual, partly tactile, partly audible – one sees, feels and hears all at the same time; the image is reinforced by the memory of a horse being curried (the same sounds, etc.). Three sensations together – that makes for strength in writing. In painting one can have the same multiple sensations. A colour harmony is a visual sensation. But it can be combined with a three-dimensional form, and then one has a tactile sensation (*as if* one could touch the form). One can also have the illusion of movement (as in Marcel Duchamp). But the reaction must always be *sensational* – not intellectual and not necessarily symbolic. The symbol is not sensational, but emotional, and is therefore *not necessarily* a work of art. Perhaps a work of art gains another dimension, an extra *frisson*, through being an archetype. But *sensation d'abord!*

I read through your letter again in the train, and what pleased me best was the sense of a recovered morale. It seemed like a letter from someone beginning a new life in a new world. That is wonderful, and I hope it lasts, and gets into your pictures. Art, as I have said before, is always a *Bejahung* – an affirmation of wonder and enjoyment. Don't think I cannot appreciate your sense of loneliness and insecurity – your *déracinement*, etc. But you will lose

\* Stendhal's metaphor, in a somewhat different context.

that once you have made a world of your own – you will create your own foundations, smooth the rock on which to stand; and that will give you the sense of new found land.

Gabo feels exactly as you do, and has often spoken to me about it. He, too, is a Jew, who loved his Russia and has never been at home anywhere else in the world (he felt best in England). That is why he talks so often of 'a new reality', and that is perhaps his real reason for trying to create an art that has no relation to any known landscape or natural phenomenon. The world does not appreciate yet what he is trying to do. He is not advocating that a constructive work of art should consist merely of an arrangement of elemental means of expression for no other purpose than to let them speak for themselves. 'I am constantly demanding from myself and keep on calling to my friends, not to be satisfied with that gratifying arrangement of elemental shapes, colours, and lines for the mere gratification of arrangement; I demand that they shall remain only means for conveying a well-organized and clearly defined image – not just some image, any image, but a new and constructive image by which I mean one which by its very existence as a plastic vision should provoke in us the forces and the desires to enhance life, assert it and assist its further development.'*

* 'On Constructive Realism.' *Three Lectures on Modern Art*. New York (Philosophical Library), 1949, p. 83.

You see, he is wonderfully optimistic, wonderfully positive. He is, I think, the most inspiring person I have ever known: to know him is to believe in him, apart from any theories he may have of what he is trying to do.

Mondrian was a very different type. He was a mystic—a man of very simple habits, living like a saint in a viewless room he had painted white. He hated nature, but he loved dancing (jazz). He hated the personality—perhaps he hated life. But he believed in the absolute, the pure, in perfection. He wished to exclude all accidents from art, all sensibility. He wanted an art of pure intuition, of perfect measure. He was the opposite of an expressionist; he owed nothing to his unconscious (except perhaps his drive); everything to his sensibility. He would spend weeks painting one small area of colour, to get the right degree of intensity. He always worked to a millimetre of precision, registered by his eye alone.

You are not so intuitive in your art. You base your art on feeling, your personal and subjective feelings. You cannot be objective and 'pure' in the manner of Mondrian or Gabo, but your art becomes 'significant' (and therefore of more than personal interest) because you allow the unconscious to come through and be expressed in archetypal images. Feeling is like that, very *ur*, expressed in *Urgestalten*, forms which the artist does not consciously control. Such art is the creation of *forms symbolic of human feeling.* In that sense it is *topologie,* and Tapié is correct in using such a word. It may also be erotic, but there is nothing 'mystic' about it. Tapié should not use this word – it comes from the vocabulary of charlatans!

Intuitive, or symbolic of feeling, all art must nevertheless be sensuous (sensual, if that word is more pleasing). If works of art are not sensuous, they are merely illustrations; not symbols, but semantic signs (words, mathematical diagrams, etc.).

The sensuous in art is all that is virile, vitalistic, life-enhancing. It is this quality that Matisse possessed so abundantly, but because he is comparatively inhibited (i.e. afraid of the unconscious) he does not use it in the service of feelings that are significant enough. But one should not despise such an artist, for such 'beauty' is not merely on the surface, external. As style, skill, *flair, verve,* etc., it comes from the senses. One cannot be an artist without possessing such a sensuous organism.

But we also have need to give form to our intuitions – Susanne Langer's definition of art as 'the creation of forms symbolic of human feeling' is too narrow. But feeling is the basic thing – the scope of intuition is much more limited, and there isn't the same urgent need to express it.

In your letter you return to the question of colour, and almost accuse me of having misled you! You say that colour is connected with nature, and that the only thing which now binds you with nature is *light* and *mood*. But light is colour, or colour light. Otherwise it is merely an abstraction, and not natural. What you mean, is again a sculptor's point of view. Gabo finds colour so antipathetic that he even avoids black and white, and makes his constructions in transparent materials like glass and plastic. I think this is legitimate for pure form, but your other element, *mood*, is not pure in this sense. It is subjective, and is expressed in symbols; and every mood has its symbolic equivalent in colour or colour-harmonies. In other words, there is no point in using paint as a medium of expression unless you exploit its characteristic quality, which is colour.

But admittedly, black and white are also colours. Soulages, Kline, Saura and those people who paint only in black and white, although they often make wonderfully rich 'chords' of colour (like the bass notes of a piano), are terribly oppressive in the mass. You see one painting and like it, but if you see twenty together it is like a funeral procession.

All colours are symbolic. Black is the colour of despair, of nihilism. It is the colour of concepts, of ideas – not of feelings and sensations. It is a medium for *illustration*, not for *creation*.

The *réel* cannot be *dévidé* – that is the fundamental mistake behind Tapié's philosophy of art. It assumes that there is a pre-existing reality which has only to be discovered, expressed. But that is not true. Reality is something which we *construct* out of the chaos of our sense-impressions. Reality may look rather like a Pollock to a newly-born child, but then begins a long process of learning – a process of testing, arranging, measuring, creating. Creating a coherent world of vision and imagination; creating the symbols by means of which we can communicate this coherence. Always exploring and building – that is the specifically human activity, and the specifically artistic activity is to define (make definite and clear) this constructed reality, and to extend the area of coherent consciousness, to find new symbols for refinements of feeling. And always there should be the sense of positive achievement, of conquest, of *Bejahung*. That is why to my way of thinking an artist like Gabo is immeasurably greater than any of these 'informalists' or surrealists. He is creative in the only real sense of the word – he brings a new concrete and objective *fact* into existence; he does not merely unwind a tangled skein from his own guts. The following, which I read in a book by Jaspers last night, is *à propos*:

'There is often an element of wizardry in great minds. To be skilled in magic is often a great gift. Some of the great phenomena of German Idealism belong to this sphere; for example, Fichte's description of his own age as a turning-point and of his own philosophy as the crucial achievement of this turning-point. And the same pattern recurs in Nietzsche. Nietzsche's prophetic vision wavers awkwardly between deep insight and fraudulent deception. Marx's eschatology has the same fundamental flaw. But what is an obsession, an objective sub-jectivism in these great men *is merely disgusting in smaller minds*: the tendency to declare one's own thinking absolute, the only true thinking, *egocentrically to identify oneself with the object,* and to reject whatever conflicts with one's own interest and ideas. Such minds look not for friends but for admirers and obedient followers. They assess everyone purely according to the potential contribution he can make to their own self-aggrandizement.

'*But one single person is never merely a magician* and not one of us is impervious to the seductions of magic . . . the magician does not know what he is doing nor how he is doing it . . . the magician examines not so much the truth as his own gestures, modes of expression and ways of impressing others. . . . The magician refuses to have his truth put to the test; he seems to be blind to the difference be-tween truth and untruth, reality and appearance. He cannot really converse with others; he cannot engage in a candid discussion. He is biassed by his ideas, both by those he forms for himself and those he takes over. He goes through life a personification of the will to power, never seeing through his own motives.'

Now we know why Tapié talks so much of '*magie*'! Jaspers is describing magic in philosophy, but it is the same in art, and all these words are true of Pollock, Mathieu *et cie*. They avoid form because form is an objective truth to which they will not submit their precious personalities. But they do not even believe in their own personalities, in the sense of anything dignified and reasonable. They are simply nihilists.

I can never say much in the immediate presence of a painting – they are symbols which must speak directly to us, and analysis must come afterwards as a slow and boring business. But I am excited by what I see in your work – or rather, apprehensive. What you are trying to do is terribly difficult, and one does not even know whether it is completely possible. You are climbing up the narrow ridge between the conscious and the unconscious, and as you know in such a situation one must not look down, or even to the side, but always to the front. It is a long, long climb, and all the while you tremble as if about to make a revelation – one sees the forms beating against some last veil. With only a degree more 'realization' the forms will be complete, the symbol will be created.

I think you still do too much 'doodling' *on the canvas* instead of making preliminary sketches. This leads to *une facture fatiguée,* to incoherence in the design. This may be because your preliminary conceptions of colour are not precise enough. When you make a drawing or a gouache, the *forms* are perfectly precise; then you begin to translate them into colour on the canvas, and you grow unsure of them, because the colours do not seem to match up to the forms as you had conceived them. But the colours should be just as much predetermined as the forms.

When one sees the drawings of old masters, they often have precise indications of colour written on them. I know that Matisse and Picasso have described another way of painting, building up from the first splash of colour, working mosaic-fashion (as Riopelle must do), but this is for a different kind of painting, not for formal paintings like yours. You remember La Fresnaye's *Homme assis*? – such a painting is conceived like an architect's plan – it is *a harmonic calculation*, the very opposite of doodling. Leave doodling to Mathieu and Michaux – paint like La Fresnaye, Gris, Delaunay, Marcel Duchamp. That is not an old-fashioned way of painting – it is the universal and only essential way. Human perception eventually rejects every other way of painting. Perception must crystallize into a significant form before it can become a symbol for our feelings.

\*　　　　\*　　　　\*

I was very interested in your account of Romegger's visit. Yes, of course, you have complexes, and so have I, and so have many people who are not artists. I don't believe that the question of *being an artist* has anything to do with complexes – certainly not the question of being a *good* artist. The quality of art is much more in the senses, in perception and sensational reflexes; in our reactions (physical) to colour and shape and sound. So you are right about the Sartre story. Whether it reveals an Oedipus complex in Sartre or not has nothing at all to do

43

with the question of whether or not it is a good story. The goodness of the story is a question of dramatic structure, of verbal felicity, and of the human emotions that are touched. Of course, we may admit that the emotions will be moved by the Oedipus theme, however disguised (and most moved when most subtly disguised). But other people who are not artists have these emotional complexes, and the artist is just the one who can express them for us, give them an external form which makes them more acceptable perhaps, which gets them out of the system, as we say. But it is the 'giving form', the creation of the symbol, that makes the art; and that has nothing to do with the complex as such, though the complex may provide the necessary energy to set the process going.

'Suffering' is necessary to give depth to our emotional life, to save the artist from being superficial; but it is not in itself a fit subject for art. Yeats once said: 'passive suffering is not a theme for poetry. In all the great tragedies, tragedy is a joy to the man who dies; in Greece the tragic chorus danced.' All skill is joyful, he also said, and that brings us back to what I have always meant by *Spielerei* – not so much 'play', as 'joy', *joie de vivre*. One must affirm life, not deny it.

There is another problem you asked me about –about being detached from oneself in one's work. That was answered in my Ascona lecture, and I think you really understand it perfectly. It is merely a question of not being too deliberate in the act of creation. The artist is an instrument of forces which come from the unconscious, and which are in some sense supra-personal. But it is not enough to be a passive instrument, a channel through which images are automatically expressed. That was the surrealists' mistake. The instrument must be tuned, it must be *expressive*, and it can be expressive only through formal (i.e. aesthetic) means. These are universal qualities, but only the artist is sensitive to them, or the artist in us all (because there must be response as well as expression). So there are really two universal and non-personal aspects of art – its unconscious symbolic aspect, and its formal aesthetic aspect. The 'person' is the point in which they meet.

Significantly, I too work in this way – not like a scholar who accumulates his facts and then makes a theory about them. But rather as you paint a picture – I plunge into the subject, swim about for the facts, and find the theory. I know only vaguely what I want to write about (for that reason I always find it difficult to give a title to an article or a book until it is written), but I have a real hunch. I know, for example, that no one has yet shown how art *evolves*. They say it does not evolve – that it depends on economic conditions or spiritual forces. But I know instinctively that that is not true. It is an organic force, *un élan créateur*, and over thousands of years it has been *expanding* – not evolving in a straight line, but sending out feelers (antennae) first in one direction and then in another, feelers that explore the darkness of *Nichts*, the limits of perception. It does these things because it is biologically necessary if man is to evolve: he has to become more sensitive to his environment, to get a firmer grasp on reality. And one grasps reality by the senses, not by the intellect. The only reality is that first established by poets and artists. That is what Hölderlin saw so clearly—Schiller and Schelling, too. There is a wonderful poem of Hölderlin's, *Wie wenn am Feiertage*, which is too long to quote, but the idea is in lines like these:

Und wie im Aug' ein Feuer dem Manne glänzt,
Wenn hohes er entwarf; so ist
Von neuem an den Zeichen, den Taten der Welt
    jetzt
Ein Feuer angezündet in Seelen der Dichter.
Und was zuvor geschah, doch kaum gefühlt,
Ist offenbar erst jetzt,
Und die uns lächelnd den Acker gebauet,
In Knechtsgestalt, sie sind erkannt,
Die Allebendigen, die Kräfte der Götter.*

---

* And as a fire gleams in the eye of that man who has conceived a noble design; so now once again by the signs, the deeds of the world a fire has been kindled in the souls of the poets. And what came to pass before, though scarcely felt, only now is manifest, and they who smiling tended our fields for us, in the guise of labourers, now have been recognized, the all and ever living, the powers of the gods'. (Trans. Michael Hamburger: *Hölderlin*, Penguin Poets.)

When man found he could make a living image of the animal he had to kill, when he first made an abstract pattern for which there was no image in nature – these were decisive moments in the evolution of his consciousness, in his mental and spiritual development. Man made an image and then worshipped it. That is how religion began. In the beginning was the Image, and the Image was God! An African anthropologist told me that even to-day when a native makes an image of a thing – a drawing or a statue – it is more real to him than his vision of the thing. The image he has made has more power than the thing it represents. One has always to find new ways of saying this – one has to go on repeating and repeating the truth, in simpler and always simpler ways. But people's minds are like a glass of Pernod – they go cloudy if you pour words into them.

One is too impatient. One must wait – wait on things. A new volume of Simone Weil's *Cahiers* has been published. Here is a Taoist text, attributed to Lao Tzu, which much impressed her – she refers to it two or three times:

'To destroy locusts in full flight, it is enough simply to see in the whole universe the particular locust aimed at and nothing more: you cannot then fail to hit it. To become an archer, you should lie for two years under a loom and not blink your eyes when the shuttle darts back and forth; then for three years, with your face turned to the light, make a louse climb up a silk thread. When the louse appears to be larger than a wheel, than a mountain; when it hides the sun; when you see its heart, you may then shoot: you will hit it right in the middle of the heart.'

Many good things on *travail* and *attention*, 'L'habitude d'un travail procure une possession du monde. *Habitude* dans le travail. Elimination du "je". Image de la parfaite vertu.'

But 400 pages of such sayings! *Sans ordre, pêle-mêle.* What is most striking, and a little terrifying, is the *fever* of her thoughts. Where does it lead her? Perhaps only to silence.

To silence! I now feel that I have said all I have to say to you about the art of painting – about *your* art of painting in *our* time. One day you confessed that you felt the futility of so much that is written on art in view of the fact that the level of consciousness in the interpretation or criticism of art can never be the level of the creative consciousness. Only the artist himself, in some rare moments, can bridge such a gap.

I agree. I would not write to you about your painting, nor indeed would I venture to write about art of any kind, unless I could believe that I also write as an artist, and not as a layman (I have no ambition to write about art as an historian or a philosopher.) I am impelled to write about the plastic arts because I am a poet, and if you retort (as many of my critics are ready to do) that it would be more seemly to write about my own craft, then I must explain that there are two reasons why for the most part I prefer to write about painting – perhaps three, if one may suggest that in their inarticulateness, artists need poets as their interpreters. But the impelling reasons are these: first, we live in an age when poetry has lost its force. It exists, like a submerged stream, and those who are thirsty for it can occasionally tap it. In this situation the poet seeks other outlets, and one of the most appealing of them is the interpretation of other arts. That he sometimes succeeds, even to the satisfaction of the artist, is sufficiently proved by such writers as Ruskin, Baudelaire and Pater. The other reason is perhaps more difficult to formulate. I believe that the great tragedy of the present century is a tragedy of separation, or alienation: man's lips have fallen from the breast of Nature, his mother Nature, and most of his anxieties and aggressiveness spring from this fact. How can man be brought back to a direct sensuous relationship with Nature? Only, I believe, through the arts, and above all through those arts, like painting and sculpture, which give him, by manipulation and sensuous involvement, a direct contact with natural materials.

Well, that is a point of view which I can't begin to justify at the end of this long letter, and I offer it only as an expression of why I, for one, rush in where angels like yourself fear to tread. Poets are perhaps clumsy when they come into the artist's studio – we seize on complicated instruments like psychology and use them without tact. But we are well-meaning, and – since the artist himself is so inarticulate – there is no one else who can so sympathetically, and so truly, interpret his work. 'Interpret' is not quite the right word – in some sense we add to it, extend it. As Proust said, our lives are encumbered with innumerable 'negatives' that remain useless because the intelligence has not 'developed' them. He meant the intelligence of the artist, of course, but that is my meaning too: only I see the poet and the painter working together to reveal 'the qualitative difference there is in the way we look at the world' – a difference, Proust added, that without art would remain forever each man's personal secret.

The way you look at the world is not the way Proust looked at the world – or Cézanne, or Vermeer, or any other artist he may have had in mind. But he would have admitted the infinite variety of those qualitative differences of vision represented by the history of art. What a fantastic phantasmagoria it is, from Sumer and Assyria, Egypt and Greece, down all the centuries to our own inverted way of looking at the world. We have turned our gaze inwards, and still, like Lao Tzu's archer, blink our eyes as the shuttle of swift images shoots back and forth. But eventually we shall get near to the heart of the mystery, the heart of the louse, and then our art will be an image of perfect virtue.

So much is a question of naïve belief, and your work must conform to your belief. The essence of created things, Simone Weil was always repeating, is to be intermediaries – intermediaries toward each other, and eventually toward God. I think she had a more perfect idea of the work of art as intermediary than either Ruskin or Tolstoy or any of her predecessors (except perhaps Plato) because she did not conceive the work of art as a formal communiqué, as the restatement in emotive language of a truth pre-established by science or ethics. She found the essence of a work of art in its unstated intuitions: as the movement between two established points. The most beautiful kind of music, she said, is that which gives the maximum intensity to a moment of silence, which constrains the listener to listen to the silence. First the inner silence, in between the notes; then the outer silence which is added, where the descent is one of love. She found the same double descending movement in Greek sculpture, and suggested that this double descent of silence is the key to all art. The concept is difficult, but it is true: art creates the moment when some notion of a transcendental reality becomes possible, an interval arched like a bridge between two points of sensuous reality, ascent and descent, a harmony which some people call beauty and others love.

Part II

THE AMBIGUOUS CRITIC

# THE AMBIGUOUS CRITIC

THE WORLD of art is a world without justice. One has only to contrast the miserable lives of some of the founders of the modern movement – in particular, Gauguin's and Van Gogh's – with the present high estimation given to their works, to appreciate the injustice of a situation that has always prevailed since art became an affair between an individual and a patron. The patron knows no laws beyond those of his own vanity and desires; and the individual artist is completely dependent on the patron's whims. Between the dependent artist and the independent patron there can intervene only those arbitrary laws of supply and demand which characterize our capitalist system, which are not laws in any moral or judicial sense, but rather blind forces governed by hope or fear. The economic 'laws' governing the distribution and sale of works of art only differ from the laws governing the distribution and sale of bacon by the relative scarcity of the artistic product, and by the relative ease with which the market can be controlled.

These generalizations, and those that follow, apply to the capitalist world; in authoritarian states the artist is subject to less arbitary forces. He sacrifices his freedom and his individuality and in exchange is given economic security. The artist in Russia or in China may by now have been conditioned to a mental outlook in which 'to paint' or 'to write' means to work according to acceptable specifications, as did the artists of the Middle Ages in Europe. I have had long discussions with painters and writers in China, and though I realized that my contacts were preselected, there was no doubt that Chinese artists enjoy an economic security unknown to the artists of the West, and would regard ideological freedom as a poor exchange for such security. But as a matter of fact (fact which does not alter the question of principle involved) Chinese painters, under a wide umbrella called 'traditional art', enjoy a degree of freedom denied to their Russian colleagues, simply because their tradition is rich in alternative styles of expression.

To enlighten the blind forces that control art in a capitalist world, various institutions have been established which attempt to give disinterested recognition to merit. Of these the official academies are the oldest and still perhaps the most powerful. But in every country they tend, in the course of time, to become self-renewing oligarchies – that is to say, bodies that admit only like-minded members, and their standards are always conservative. In revolt against such reactionary 'establishments', from time to time 'secessions' and 'free academies' have been established, but these again in their turn become conservative, defending the taste of a generation against new-comers. The official academies survive because they are privileged and often receive state support; the 'secessions' die and are renewed. But in all this ceaseless institutional warfare no legality is established. Institutions exist to defend sectional interests; least of all does the state ever succeed in exercising objective judgement.

Institutions usually exert their influence on the general public through exhibitions. Exhibitions are the open markets where art is bought, and it is possible, of course, to organize exhibitions that are independent of institutions. Dealers in art are of many kinds—some of them are intermediaries who function without a gallery or a registered office. Some of them are rich and famous, others struggling and obscure, but all of them regard the work of art as a commodity, to be sold to the highest bidder. All take a substantial commission when a transaction is effected.

This trade, like any other in the capitalist world, functions on capital, credit and profit, and publicity is its life blood. There are two kinds of publicity, and they thrive best if they maintain an apparent independence. One is gratuitous and haphazard; the other is planned and paid for. To establish an artist's reputation there must first exist a modicum of talent. Many bad artists have been artificially boosted, and acquired a temporary fame, but the keener the competition the closer the scrutiny. In general, collectors will not patronize an artist boosted by the trade unless there is an independent support from the critics. There are collectors who boast of their independent judgement: their cupboards are full of skeletons. There are collectors who have had courage and taken risks: they have usually at least one critic on their side.

The market is international – increasingly so as art itself becomes more and more international in style. There are dealers who operate within the frontiers of their own country, but increasingly they seek agents, representatives or collaterals in every country where there is a market for art. Some combinations have endless ramifications, at one end a financial corporation, at the other end scores of private agents who receive a commission for any introductions that lead to sales. Within the ethics of capitalism, there is nothing reprehensible in all this.

But what of the critics in this commercial network? They too are concerned with the establishment of reputations, and on their activities may depend the success or failure of an artist. It is probably true to say that the *financial* status of a contemporary artist is strictly concordant with his *critical* status, though there may be a time-lag between the two: some critics may be in advance of the market. At any rate, as in all the arts, the artist and his critics have to establish the public by which they are judged – and bought – and this takes time.

An 'Art Market Letter' dated July 1, 1960, issued by an unusually frank New York dealer, reports the following 'May and June News':

'On May 20th and 21st, the big semi-annual *auction* took place at the *Stuttgarter Kunstkabinett*, Stuttgart, Germany. There had been considerable speculation about the results of this sale, primarily because of the presence of a number of fine *Paul Klee* oils and water-colors from the Richard Doetsch-Benziger collection. Klees of this quality have rarely come on the market in recent years, despite the artist's prolific output. And because Klee prices have an important bearing on the general art market, everybody was waiting to see what they would bring. As expected, the high prices for Klee oils, which had reached close to the $50,000 price level in private transactions, were further confirmed by the auction. Other works, in addition to the Klees, brought high prices, which points up the fact that sophisticates buy at auctions only when they have to; public competition usually causes much higher prices than can be obtained in private transactions. . . . We have also listed the price of the *Bernard Buffet*, if only to shock recent purchasers of his work at the $5,000 and $6,000 level into the realization that there are such things as absolute, intrinsic values in art, and publicity does not create them.'

This is an admission of the decisive effect of the critic's intervention in the art market, and an unsolicited tribute to the integrity of critics. It is possible that some critics (I have no certain information on the subject) are secretly subsidized by dealers to boost particular artists, but other critics are likely to detect such tactics and to react more strongly than they might otherwise have done against a false reputation. In general the establishment of the kind of reputation that commands 'the $50,000 price level' is a long battle for the truth, and that level is usually reached only after the artist's death. It is exceptional for any artist to reach even the $5,000 price level before the age of fifty.

The dealer I have quoted then indulges in 'predictions', tips for the prospective buyer or investor. 'Look for big increases during the next year in the works of French surrealist André Masson, particularly the period 1927–1948. His influence on Jackson Pollock is becoming more widely recognized by connoisseurs every day. Masson is still the least expensive of the major twentieth-century artists, but this won't last long. Max Ernst prices will also spurt any moment now. They have doubled in the last year, and should do so again before the Museum of Modern Art retrospective.' And so on. Dealers in Paris or London may not be quite so blatant in their propaganda, but the same market gossip circulates everywhere.

The tip about the Museum of Modern Art 'retrospective' points to the position occupied by respectable institutions in this commercial jungle. To achieve a 'retrospective' at the Museum of Modern Art or at one of the Biennales is to reach the $50,000 level in one leap. It cannot be that the institutions in question are ignorant of the part they play in boosting market values, but their motives are surely disinterested. At least, I find it difficult to believe that any combination of dealers' craft or critics' lobbying can effect the decisions of the eminent officials who direct the institutions in question. But at this point one touches the subtlest aspects of the whole situation–the subliminal effects of publicity on all open minds.

The opinions we all hold–to what extent are they our own, arrived at by independent processes of thought? Only a rash and very conceited critic would claim that he has not, perhaps unconsciously, been influenced by all he has read about this or that artist, by the exhibitions that have been presented with such flair, by soaring prices and public acclaim. An invisible pressure works on our sensibilities all the time, and it would call for inhuman powers to resist it. All one can do is to try and keep a sense of proportion and test every reputation on innocent nerves.

The most difficult task in life is to keep an incorrupt consciousness–perhaps only the genius can succeed. Who in the past history of art criticism has succeeded in this—not Ruskin, not Baudelaire, not Roger Fry (to name only the greatest)—they all made mistakes of judgement based on prejudice (another word for a corrupt consciousness).

I have served on many juries for art prizes, with growing uneasiness. It is not that I question the competitive spirit that leads to the organization of exhibitions and prizes—they have always existed, even in Ancient Greece, and the recognition of merit has been the natural desire of every type of society. But obviously the effects of prize-giving vary according to the nature of the society within which the prizes are distributed. I do not imagine that the generous prizes given to artists in communist countries are wholly without bad effects—they are, in the first place, awarded by bureaucrats, who always as a class have bad taste, and they inevitably create jealousy and mutual distrust among artists. Artists who do not succeed in obtaining prizes or other forms of official recognition are thereby deprived of any chance of survival—there is no free market in a totalitarian society in which they can establish themselves by their individual efforts. In a capitalist society, on the other hand, the operations of the so-called 'art market' are anything but free. The work of art becomes a commodity subject to all the wiles of the unscrupulous speculator, and in this jungle warfare the award of a prize may be a weapon of decisive importance. Any jury that awards a prize is therefore in a very invidious position—it is not merely making an award for merit: it is making decisions that affect the whole 'price-structure' of the art market.

If a jury's decision had the value of absolute judgements, I do not think this would matter much—it would still be virtue that was rewarded, however unfair the distribution of the awards (for virtue, as we know, should be its own reward). But in effect, however genuinely and strenuously a jury strives for justice, some law of averages intervenes to produce a result that is neither just nor perhaps even desired by the jury. We may suppose five honourable critics assembled to make their choice. Each may have a different candidate, based on intimate knowledge of the artist's work. But four members of the jury will be relatively ignorant of the work recommended by the fifth member (this is especially so on international juries), with the result that in the end a majority of the jury will agree to give the prize on the basis of the highest common denominator of their knowledge. Every member of the jury is of the opinion that this artist is inferior to *his* candidate, but a majority can agree that he is the best second-best. I have discovered no system of avoiding such compromise decisions—the only solution is a jury of one!

What, then, is the duty of the disinterested critic? Should he renounce the whole system of competitions and prizes, and pursue a lonely path

63

of rectitude? It would be too simple and too falsely heroic to make the gesture of washing his hands in public and then to retire to an ivory tower. He would thereby cease to be a critic. If he is to exercise his talent in any direction whatsoever (even in disdain) he will inevitably influence opinion, and in influencing opinion, influence prices. He may conclude in such circumstances that the logic of the situation demands that he should engage in the cultural mêlée, content to raise his standard of rectitude, even if in vain.

But he may also conclude that part of his duty is to end a system so inherently unjust. 'The true mission of art is subversive', says M. Jean Dubuffet,* and the critic should be concerned 'to expose the basic challenge to authority inherent in any work of art.' That belief has always been implicit and often expressed in my own criticism. The art of to-day, I have always maintained, is an art of protest – protest against a barbarous civilization that is indifferent to all spiritual and aesthetic values. But however strongly we hold this opinion, there remains a practical problem that is not evaded by cynicism. The artist must live. Perhaps M. Dubuffet believes that he should live by means other than painting – by growing grapes, driving a

* In a letter to the author dated 23 March 1959, which received considerable publicity at the time, M. Dubuffet was refusing my invitation to participate in a collective exhibition from which a jury would select a painting to be awarded a prize of two million lire.

taxi-cab, teaching in a school. Poets are driven to such compromises, so why should not painters follow their virtuous example? The answer is to be found in the glittering prizes which do nevertheless hang on the painter's horizon (but not on the poet's). Surely even M. Dubuffet does not disdain to accept the market price for his subversive paintings. In other words, we cannot immediately contract out of the civilization we live in – Gauguin tried the experiment, with doubtful success, and in any case, there are no primitive islands left in the world. Our necessary compromise, therefore, is to live with the world we find ourselves born into, and at the same time make our necessary work a challenge to that world – in other words, we practise a certain deception, using the corrupt channels of competitive enterprise to carry the poison that will slowly but surely corrode the system. But let us not pretend that our deception is honourable. There is no possibility of honour, of decency, or of a great art until we have established a society in which art is no longer a trade, and artists no longer the creators of 'market commodities'.

## THE CRITIC'S CHOICE

'AN INVISIBLE PRESSURE works on our sensibilities all the time. . . . All one can do is to try and keep a sense of proportion and test every reputation on innocent nerves.'

Thus I have written on a preceding page, and I now intend to expose my innocence by reprinting some appreciations of contemporary artists which have been occasionally published in past years. It is necessary to understand the origins of such brief tributes. Almost all of them were written on the request either of the artist himself, or his dealer, or some organization like the British Council. I am not, therefore, directly responsible for the choice of these artists, though no doubt my general preferences are known to those who have approached me. Like any other critic, I am often pressed to write such prefaces, usually for the catalogue of an exhibition. In order to reduce the demands to manageable proportions – to accede to all of them would be impossible – I make a rule to write only about artists who are known to me personally, and whose work I have seen evolving over a number of years. It is not a professional activity – neither the dealer nor the artist pays me for such services. The selection is piecemeal and hazardous; the response is spontaneous and in no sense represents an order of merit.

In the circumstances for which they are designed, such prefaces should be appreciative rather than critical – when you are introducing a friend to a gathering of strangers, you do not draw attention to the wart on his nose, or even mention his domestic difficulties. In these short articles, which are rarely read by those who visit an exhibition (sometimes in desperation another critic takes from them a priming for his invective) I have tried to work towards a new prose form: nothing so ambitious as a poem in prose, but a composition which should not be lacking in grace, and which should create a mood – the mood in which the artist's work is accessible. I cannot pretend that I have often succeeded in this aim, but I think it is perhaps worth while to rescue a few of the pieces from oblivion, rather in the manner in which I have seen flowers rescued from a banqueting table, and taken home by the last guests. By now some of the bouquets have faded, and some that still look fresh may be artificial.

These artists therefore are the prickly thorns of his dilemma rather than 'a critic's choice'. This is the title which a London gallery gives to an annual exhibition, inviting a critic to make his own selection of the works to be shown to the public – in other words, to make a public confession of his taste. I was the invited critic in 1956 and some remarks I made on that occasion may now serve as an apology for the random names that follow in this book:

'In the past twenty-five years I have written much about contemporary art, but generally with a philosophical or perhaps sometimes a psychological intention. I have tried to be as objective as possible, and have deliberately refrained from confusing a would-be scientific activity with any expression of my likes and dislikes. For this reason I have occasionally been accused of having no direct relation to the work of art as such – of being, that is to say, an intellectualist without any sensuous response to aesthetic values.

'I suppose there are theorists of art who work with their nerves carefully insulated – I have known, historians of art who always use photographs for their researches and feel uncomfortable when confronted with an original painting! But that has not been my method of work. I have lived among artists and have had the privilege of close friendship with some of the leading painters and sculptors of my time. I have visited hundreds of studios and exhibitions in many parts of the world, and have always realized that a theory of art must be based, not only on a knowledge of the history of art, but also on a close contact with the contemporary practice of it. Only in this way can a critic appreciate the miracle of transformation that takes place in the actual *process* of creation.

'On this occasion, however, I am to abdicate my role of objectivity and freely declare my personal tastes! I accept the challenge with some trepidation – because my freedom is so carefully circumscribed. I am limited to less than thirty paintings, and to about half a dozen artists. More seriously, I am limited to living British artists, and even within that category, to artists of certain age limits. How comparatively easy my task would have been if I could have expressed my personal choice from the works of Renoir and Vuillard, Braque and Klee, or any of a dozen artists to whom I am passionately devoted, but who are beyond the imposed pale! How 'safe' my revealed taste would then have seemed, how sensuous and serene! But I have no such liberty, and must turn my eyes to the contemporary scene in England.

'One further limitation is self-imposed. I have been preceded by another critic, Mr Eric Newton, and at least two of the painters he chose might have competed for a place in my ideal exhibition. I have deliberately excluded these painters because it seemed to me that the field was wide enough for two critics to avoid each other's tracks. In other words, my choice has been to that extent restricted by what is perhaps an irrelevant sense of fairness.

'Now for some explanation of my final selection of paintings. It will at once be seen by anyone who visits the exhibition that they all tend towards that extreme in contemporary art which is known as 'abstraction', and this will immediately reinforce the already prevalent suspicion of an intellectual approach to art. I must insist, therefore, that I *like* this kind of art – that it gives me a directly sensuous and profound enjoyment. Let me be as emphatic as possible on this point: I do not intend this exhibition to be another demonstration in the bitter conflict between realism and abstraction in modern art. I follow the dictates of my own sensibility alone, and this exhibition is the result.

'I have in the past written much about abstraction in general, and this is not the place for a philosophical discourse. What must be reaffirmed, however, is that the kind of art misrepresented by the word "abstraction" is neither "formalist" nor "pure" nor "academic" in the perjorative senses of these words. It differs from so-called realist art (again an ambiguous term – used generally to indicate expressionist art with a class-conscious scope) in that it accepts as realistic the constituent elements of the medium of expression. This is to say, the realistic elements of the art of painting are: *paint* as a plastic substance of infinite variations of surface and tone; *formal relations* as a reflection of the essential nature of the real world; and *intuitive vision* as the artist's power to create a symbolic discourse of universal validity. The vision is, of course, the first necessity, for without it the artist cannot exploit his medium as a formal and plastic language. Granted this vision, this creative power of expression, he can communicate to us a consciousness of the nature of reality far more profound than any that is present in the representation of the superficial appearance of objects.

'*To live in the realm of forms* (Cassirer has said) *does not signify an evasion of the issues of life; it represents, on the contrary, the realisation of one of the highest energies of life itself.*

'I know that in identifying realism with the "superficial appearance of objects" I am begging the question. I shall be told that the effort of every realist since Cézanne (if not since Masaccio) has been to get beneath the superficial appearance of objects, to reveal the inner structure of things, to realize, as Cézanne said, the structure of what we actually see. But Cézanne's aim, rigorously followed, has led step by step with inexorable logic to the kind of painting I have chosen for this exhibition.'

It only remains to give the names of the artists I freely chose on that occasion: Ben Nicholson, Victor Pasmore, Alan Davie, Peter Kinley, Patrick Heron and William Scott. Five years later I do not find myself regretting that choice, but I am ruefully aware of the fact that given another chance to-day, I might revise the list, not because any one of these artists has failed to maintain his painterly virtues, but because in myself I have felt that invisible pressure which is not so much a yielding to forces outside oneself, as the thrust of growth within.

## BEN NICHOLSON · FRANCIS BACON
## LUCIEN FREUD

THAT Ben Nicholson and Francis Bacon belong to distinct generations may be a sufficient explanation of their diversity. Ben Nicholson, born in 1894, spent the decisive years of youth in what might be called an Age of Revelation – the age in which new images of reality were first discovered and presented to the world, the age of cubism, futurism, constructivism and neo-plasticism. Francis Bacon, born in 1910, grew up in an Age of Disillusion, for which the brave new images of abstract art seemed a remote fantasy, alien and unexpressive,

I can write with more sympathy for Ben Nicholson's art because I too belong to that Age of Revelation, and can still believe that positive symbols – symbols of beauty or harmony – are the only answer to despair. In the unthinking days before the First World War beauty was its own excuse – it was a spontaneous expression of joyful living, or, on a higher plane perhaps, a spiritual reconciliation to the tragedy of death. The note was lyrical, and Ben Nicholson grew up in an atmosphere of lyricism – his father was an exquisite painter in the Whistlerian manner. Some of the son's early landscapes and

*Ben Nicholson Piazza della Cathedrale 1958*

*Francis Bacon  Magdalene  1946*

*Lucien Freud Interior at Paddington 1951*

*Piet Mondrian Rhythm of Straight Lines 1935-48*

still-lifes show no violent departure from this tradition. Indeed, the possibility is that a sensibility attuned in its infancy to the frail beauties of flowers and porcelain, moulded to the elegance of *art-nouveau* ornament and design, carries through to the equally refined subtleties of abstract art. The particular distinction that Ben Nicholson has given to abstract art, among all the painters of this school, is usually conveyed by such words as elegance, refinement and subtlety.

I have spoken elsewhere* of the influences that were decisive in Ben Nicholson's development – Picasso and Braque, Gris and Arp – but there can be no doubt that most decisive of all was the direct example of Piet Mondrian. I say 'direct example' to indicate that it was a question of personal inspiration, of immediate and (during Mondrian's period in London) of almost daily contact. Ben Nicholson is not and never has been a theorist, and could never be a didactic or academic artist. Mondrian was both: his writings in explanation of neo-plasticism are of a high philosophical order – no modern movement has received from one of its practitioner's a comparably clear aesthetic (and I am not forgetting the writings of Kandinsky and Klee). Mondrian aspired to create a new school of painting – a new style of art – and he went about it in the academic way, with definitions and treatises, as well as with his own masterpieces.

* Introduction to *Ben Nicholson: Paintings and Drawings*, London (Lund Humphries), 1948.

But I doubt if Ben Nicholson has read the Master's writings: for he is singularly instinctive, and he only needed, for an immediate apprehension of their significance, the visual presence of the Master's paintings.

It is probable that what Nicholson most admired in Mondrian was his probity – his purity of intention and his consistency of practice. Mondrian was a disciplinarian of almost mystical integrity. He would strive to eliminate even his own pleasure and certainly his own personality in an effort to attain to some ideal of perfect form, some statement of hitherto inconceived harmony. That aim tends to give his paintings the other-worldliness of mystical *mandalas,* whose secret attraction is precisely that the personal, the sentimental, the impulsive and sensuous self is lost in the contemplation of pure form. Nicholson's paintings have no mystical aura of this kind: as an artist he remains confidently aware of his sensations, and even his 'purest' works, the white reliefs of about 1930, depend, for appreciation, on their direct aesthetic appeal – they are still, in the Whistlerian manner, 'harmonies in white'.

Nowhere, in his now impressive achievement, does Nicholson dispense with the sensuous substance of the painter's art. He may reduce subject-matter to purely formal categories of geometrical severity; he may subdue his colour harmony to the near-zero of white and shade; but even then the whiteness has the sensuous appeal of porcelain or snow. And what is sensuous can never be wholly abstract. Nicholson's forms and colours are not conceptual or schematic: they can always be linked, however remotely, to the visible world. They are, properly speaking, a reduction of the sensible appearance of that visible world to its subtlest essence.

That is why, in spite of its consistent style, his art has such variety. It is the variety of nature, but that variety in its essential forms. Certain shapes constantly reappear in his paintings: the profile of a vase, a cup, a table, the curve of a breast; elemental shapes that are superimposed one upon another, not confusingly, not even ambiguously; but creating a formal epitome that will echo in the sensations endlessly. It is the opposite effect to that of a visual cliché. The cliché, once perceived, leaves us indifferent even if the cliché is a naked woman or a bowl of fruit. The archetypal form is never a cliché: it has a depth of reference that we cannot plumb or penetrate, a continuity of recollection that is never exhausted.

The paintings of Ben Nicholson are archetypal in this sense: wells of colour and form into which our consciousness sinks with vertiginous wonder.

That same consciousness is shocked and outraged by the paintings of Francis Bacon. This painter has no links with the serene climate that prevailed before the wars. He was born into a waste land and his work expresses a sense of bewilderment, of lost innocence. No doubt he has some affinity with the Surrealists, though it would be difficult to indicate stylistic influences derived from any one of the original animators of that international movement. The only near relationship – and it is almost wholly technical – is with Graham Sutherland, with whom Bacon worked for a short period. He has perhaps a more subjective affinity with a remoter artist – with the more spectral side of Fuseli's art; and, as in Sutherland's case, there is perhaps a suggestion of Blake's influence. But these influences are not important. With a technical facility that is almost unrivalled among his British contemporaries, he projects the terrifying images of a very private mind.

Images of the unconscious, no doubt; but not the automatic images of the Surrealists. Rather, Bacon's images are deliberate symbols. These screaming faces, these headless bodies, these curtains drawn over some sinister scene, these animals in eternal pursuit of their own tails, this prelate in a crystal cage – all these are symbols of a disintegrating world, of a paranoiac consciousness. It is a world in which the artist can find no status, no point of stability, no essential purpose. Some sympathy with the Existentialists is perhaps to be suggested – certainly with the Sartrian school of that philosophy. But the Existentialist tends to see in art an expression of human freedom – an act of constructive defiance in the face of an annihilating reality. Man's art should be an affirmation of his indomitable will to live and to create. That was Nietzsche's conception of art; and that, in his naïve way, has been Ben Nicholson's. But Bacon has no such constructive impulse. Rather he is animated by a destructive sadism, and if he affirms anything beyond his personal existence, it is the meaninglessness of the mystery of life.

Lucien Freud at first sight may seem to provide an extreme contrast both to the purism of Nicholson and to the nihilism of Bacon. But that is far from being true. His realism does not escape from the limitations of the visible world; nor does it deride that world by satire. But in subtle ways it manages to indicate its mystery – the inexplicable mystery of existence itself, in a fruit or a leaf; the mysterious individuality of a body or a face; the mysterious collocation of an individual with a plant or a flower. Again one might trace influences – the influence of Dali, perhaps, but more likely the influence of some Italian master – a Cosimo or a Leonardo. But these influences have been thoroughly assimilated and we are left with a vision that is singularly direct and disturbing in its very actuality.

Freud, who is a grandson of the famous psychologist, can hardly be claimed as a typical English artist; nor can Francis Bacon, in spite of his English ancestry. Nicholson, it seems to me, is very English; his paintings have an English complexion.

But all three artists belong to a world-wide movement – to varieties of style within that movement that are now as international as any of the political and economic movements of our time. What we now look for in art is not conformity to a doctrine, much less a uniformity of style; but, within a framework that becomes more and more universal, an expression of the individual sensibility. Each of these artists is independent in this sense; each contributes, in his individual way, to the growing reputation of English art.

# BRANCUSI

## ONE

AT THE TIME of his death in 1957 Constantin Brancusi had won an unsurpassed reputation among contemporary sculptors on the basis of a very restricted production and for qualities which had little to do with either the academic or the revolutionary movements of his time. He held himself aloof, though there was a time (between 1904 and 1914) when he associated with Modigliani, the only other sculptor who ever had anything in common with him. For the last forty years of his life he lived as a recluse in his Paris studio–a life of austerity and spiritual meditation, for he had been much influenced by Tibetan mysticism, particularly the *Milarepa*, the confessions of an eleventh-century Tibetan monk. He was always severely critical of his contemporaries; nevertheless he has been revered almost as a saint, and his work has had a profound effect on the development of modern sculpture.

He was born at Pestisani, near Turgujiu, Rumania, on 21 February, 1876, and received his first training in the local carpentry school. He won a scholarship to the Art Academy of Bucharest and having gained his diploma, made for Paris where he arrived in 1904. He was to remain there all his life, and very rarely left his studio (an exception is the visit he made to India in 1937 to design a temple of meditation for the Maharajah of Indor, a project which was never finished owing perhaps to the outbreak of war; fragments were scattered about his studio).

His early work is academic, and for a few years after his arrival in Paris he was influenced by Rodin. The decisive change in his style occurred about 1907, and is strikingly illustrated by the two versions of *La muse endormie*. The first version, of 1906, shows the sleeping face of the muse emerging from a background of roughly-hewn marble, the delicate naturalistic features contrasting with the unfinished rock. Rodin had used this device, perhaps inspired by Michelangelo's unfinished sculptures. In 1909–10 Brancusi repeated the subject, but this time all the background was carved away, the obtrusive elements of the face (nose, eyebrows and ears) reduced almost to linear indications, and thus was evolved the first of those egg-shaped carvings which are so characteristic of Brancusi's style.

In the same manner and about the same time as Picasso and other artists, Brancusi felt the impact of African tribal wood sculpture. This phase lasts from about 1914 (*Le fils prodigue* of that year now in the Arensberg Collection, Philadelphia Museum of Art) to 1925 (*Le chef* of that year), but all the time this essentially exotic influence is being tempered by Brancusi's innate classicism; gradually the negro idols are transformed into quasi-classical columns.

To use the word 'classical' to characterize the work of this revolutionary artist only shows how ambiguous such labels can be. The words that can be used without ambiguity to describe Brancusi's work are words like 'simplicity' and 'integrity', words which are not the copyright of any school or movement. 'Innocence' is perhaps another such word, and one of the most significant of the sayings attributed to Brancusi will make very clear what we mean by this word: 'When we are no longer children, we are already dead.' An innocent eye does not imply infantilism, but rather an absence of the prejudices and distortions of a civilization that separates the artist from nature. 'Simplicity is not an aim in art – one attains simplicity in spite of oneself by getting near to the real sense of things' – that further saying of Brancusi's is equally significant, and it implies an objectivity, an extra-version of sensation and thought, which separates Brancusi decisively from the expressionist schools of our time.

Only during the classical cubist period of Braque and Picasso can Brancusi be said to have belonged to the main current of modern art. But cubistic though some of his creations may be (*Le coq* of 1924, for example), there is always in Brancusi's typical work a vitalistic element which derives from the observation of nature. It may be an abstract quality of a natural object, as when he embodies the flashing swiftness of a bird's flight (*L'oiseau dans l'espace*, the five-feet-high polished bronze in Peggy Guggenheim's Collection, Venice); and even the form of the egg is vital, for all its mathematical perfection. It is almost the Platonic 'idea' of the natural object that Brancusi seems to seek to represent, and his success in this attempt gives to his work its extraordinary integrity and sense of everlastingness.

Is he then a perfect artist, like Arnold's Shakespeare, beyond 'the foil'd searching of mortality'? I do not think so. I must confess that in two or three of his works, in the famous *Mademoiselle Pogany* in particular, I am disturbed by a quality of over-sophistication, of utter refinement rather than utter simplicity. Perhaps the negroid works were a reaction from this quality, designed to correct a tendency of which the artist himself was fully conscious. There are several versions of *Mademoiselle Pogany*, spread between the years 1913 and 1931, and they show the progressive elimination of the sophisticated elements I have mentioned. But even in the final version I am still disturbed by a slick suavity wholly absent from his greatest works. It was Brancusi himself who said 'nude men in sculpture are not so beautiful as toads.'

Brancusi's sculpture lies at the still centre of modern art, radiating serenity but itself unaffected by the turmoil around it. Its strength is due to its containment of two contrary principles: that of a childlike naïvety, which looks at the world through innocent eyes; and that of a sophisticated wisdom with roots deep in the past, which teaches that the forms we see are never innocent, but always dictated by unconscious forces. Brancusi accepts existence like a child, but at the same time his intuition penetrates to the realm of essence. To give an example: a bird in flight is a visual experience that cannot be reduced to a static volume – the essence of it is a movement in space. Brancusi can represent such a subject because he has identified himself for an instant with the hurtling body of that bird, with the physical sensation of movement through measured time, and has thus been able to trace a graph of the force that impels the bird, a burnished form that cancels its apparent mass, to become a miraculous synthesis of essence and existence.

Such an achievement gives to Brancusi's art its suggestion of a primeval creation, independent of our particular age and civilization.

## ALBERTO BURRI

HUMAN SENSIBILITY, if confined to a narrow path, eventually reaches a point of satiety. The mind refuses any longer to register vivid sensations. This is particularly true of the artist's sensibility: his style may be constant, but his nerves are liable to exhaustion. The muscles with which he paints may still work, but automatically. He becomes slick: he is in danger of becoming popular.

Style can remain constant and the sensibility keen if the materials of art are changed. To discover and exploit new materials is a rare but necessary talent. Picasso, who possesses it in abundance, has changed from painting to sculpture, from sculpture to engraving, but that was not enough. He then invented a completely new type of art, the *collage*: an exercise of sensibility in terms of ready-made materials, scraps of paper, oilcloth, rags. Kurt Schwitters was another pioneer in the same extension of the frontiers of sensibility.

Burri has advanced still farther into unknown territory. He came to art with unusual qualifications: the skill of a surgeon, the experience of war and an awareness of the futility of academic conventions in the age of Hiroshima.

In a prisoner-of-war camp the only material to hand was old sacking. Burri's sensibility seized on its irregular texture, its subtle variations of tone, its capacity to stretch in vital tensions, and he began to sew pieces of this burlap into patterns – as a surgeon sews up incisions or wounds. The cicatrices were somehow expressive – of where pain had been, of where miraculous healing had taken place. But above all these seams were sensitive edges to entrancing areas of colour. The faded lettering on the sacks, a touch of scarlet sealing-wax or of gold-leaf for rich contrast, some meandering threads – by these means in the first years after the war Burri created a new world of form; and it seemed that the more degraded the raw material of his experiments, the more his sensibility was challenged and the more surely it triumphed. No purer works of art have been created by an artist in the past fifteen years.

But Burri did not remain content with this improbable victory. He passed to equally original experiments: to scorched laths of wood, to blistered panels of plastic, and now to welded and blasted sheets of metal. Whatever he does – and this is the wider aesthetic significance of his work – his sensibility dominates the intractable material, to such an extent that a transmutation takes place, an alchemical process in which rubbish is redeemed in the alembic of the artist's sensibility, to become the 'perfect body' of a work of art. I could carry this alchemical analogy much farther, for art has always been a kind of alchemy, and the work of art a 'treasure hard to attain'. The first thing to learn about art, if we would understand it, is that it is essentially such a process of transmutation, and Burri, by the very extremity of his chosen means, demonstrates this truth with an incomparable elegance.

# LYNN CHADWICK

## ONE

$A$T THE MOMENT of writing (1958) it is only
seven years since Lynn Chadwick held his first
exhibition in London. In 1956 he received the
International Prize for Sculpture at the Venice
Biennale, the highest award to which a modern
sculptor can aspire. Chadwick's rise to fame, therefore, has something spectacular about it, but there
is less cause for surprise when one learns that the
sculptor had already reached the age of forty-two
when the Venice award was made. The explanation
is simple – and significant. Like his contemporary,
Reg Butler, Chadwick served an apprenticeship in
another art, that of architecture. Not less significant
was his war-time experience as a pilot in the Fleet
Air Arm: the flying-machine is itself a work of art,
a dynamic form functioning in three-dimensional
space.

The war at an end, Chadwick decided to become
a sculptor, and his first works were constructions
that moved in space, like the airplane. No doubt
the 'mobiles' of Alexander Calder first suggested
this translation of a sensuous experience into plastic
form. 'To move in space' – that is the uniquely

modern sensation, and the one which Calder and Chadwick have endeavoured to represent in their sculpture. But a distinction must be made between the solutions of the problem made by these two artists. Calder's mobiles, for all their mechanical ingenuity, are essentially tellurian – that is to say, though they move in space, they move as swaying branches move, tremble in the air like leaves, and somewhere there is always the suggestion, either of a rooted trunk, or of a supporting ceiling. By their movement they create a spatial form, but it is a form seen in relation to the earth's surface. Chadwick's mobiles, by contrast, are aerial. Their movements are not related to trees and plants, but rather to birds and insects. In this they resemble flying-machines, and the closest parallel to them in the history of art are the drawings made by Leonardo for the mechanism of the wing of a flying-machine. Chadwick in his mobiles is not, of course, trying to make a machine that will fly, or even to study in a scientific spirit the mechanism of flight. But he begins with the same realization as Leonardo (for example, that 'a bird is an instrument working according to mathematical Law'), and realizing (as Leonardo also did) that there is a basic similarity in this respect between functioning instruments and the element of beauty in works of art, he makes a model or a paradigm to illustrate this universal principle.

A further distinction must be made. Leonardo's

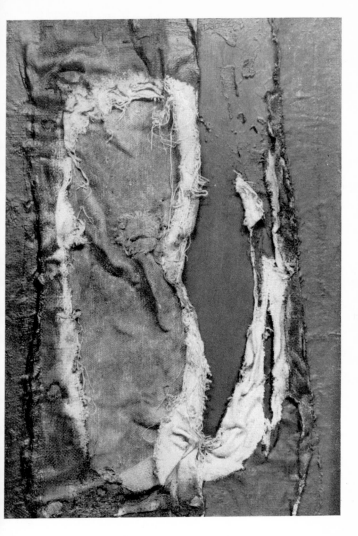

*Alberto Burri Sacco 1956*

*Lynn Chadwick  Maquette for Stranger*  1961

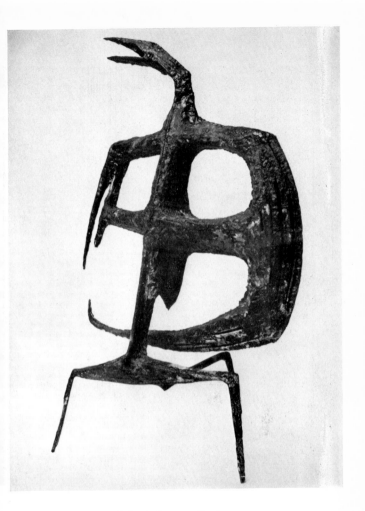

*Lynn Chadwick  Snapping Turtle  1953-54*

*Paul Delvaux The Call of the Night 1937*

drawings are scientific, strictly analytical. Their
purpose is to devitalize the bird, to arrive at a dead
machine of which man himself can become at will
'the living principle and the propeller'. But a work
of art is not a dead machine, nor can it be animated
by the intrusion of a human element, man himself.
The work of art must have its own inherent principle
of vitality. Mondrian believed that it was possible
to supply this principle from abstract sources, that
is to say, from the interplay of geometrical relationships (intuitive variations of 'the mathematical
law'). But Chadwick (by this step separating himself decisively from the Constructivists) believes
that the vitality of a work of art must be biomorphic (or, to use a more exact word, biodynamic).
That is to say, forms which strike us as dynamic,
as vital, are in the opinion of an artist like Chadwick, always related to the forms evolved by the life
force, whether in plants or animals (including the
human form). Though one of the first of his mobiles
is obviously related to airplane structures, it is
nevertheless called a 'Fish-eater' and has an
animalistic vitality.

Chadwick's 'mobile' period lasted until 1952,
and the evolutionary tendency throughout this
period of six or seven years was towards more com-
pact and more stable forms. At the same time the
animalistic element became more obvious, and in
sympathy with a now almost exclusive use of metal,
animals with a hard surface, carapaceous animals

such as beetles and crabs were the vital forms to be suggested by a universal biomorphic law.

This parallelism between nature and art should not be taken too literally. In art there are two sources of inspiration. One is found in this realm of forms which we call nature; the other is in the work of art itself. That is to say, having taken his cue or theme or motif from nature, the artist finds that he has in contemplation, not a dead and fixed idea, but one that is full of suggestions. The form lives, moves and has its being; like a cellular organism, it divides, multiplies and recombines in an almost endless series of variations. There is, that is to say, not only a form of life (form derived from nature) but also a life of forms. In the history of art, as in the development of an individual artist like Lynn Chadwick, the typical forms develop out of one another, and even when most abstract, are most vital. All these forms are held together or given unity by the artist's sense of 'style'.

The solid forms which Chadwick began to develop from 1953 onwards are an organic development of his mobiles. The basic element in sculpture has always been mass or ponderability, and though the 'space-sculpture' which a mobile defines is a legitimate variation of sculptural form, it must always remain, in relation to solid sculpture, an elegant and even an esoteric variation, if only for practical reasons, such as durability. Chadwick was searching for a technique which would combine solidity with the vitality of his metal structures, and he found it in the combination of a metal armature and a plastic composition which allows full expressive value to the bones and tendons of his figures, while at the same time giving them a 'body' with complete tactile value. The *Snapping Turtle* of 1953-4 is a transitional piece which shows the gradual thickening of the 'ossatures'. In his developed technique the underlying metal structure is no rough armature, such as is normally used in modelling, but an exactly articulated form, carefully constructed in every detail.

Having discovered an appropriate means of expression, the sculptor was free to develop what I have called his 'style'. By this ambiguous word I mean more than the formal characteristics of his work: I mean its peculiar 'ethos' or spiritual significance. Every great artist is a metaphysician. That is to say, the images he creates have a symbolic value: they are expressive of a state of mind or a feeling for which no other adequate signs or symbols exist. The artist is driven to create new signs and symbols because the degree of consciousness which they represent has not existed before, either in the evolution of human consciousness or in the history of art. On a former occasion I used a phrase to describe the symbolic significance of Chadwick's work which has been frequently quoted: the geometry of fear. I do not wish to withdraw this phrase, but it should be realized that the fear, or rather anxiety, which these works of art represent is not the fear we experience when confronted with physical peril (in a battle or an air-raid, for example). It is not the conscious fear of the dark, or even, in the animal figures, animal fear. (One must not forget that it is not the animals that express *their* fear, but the artist who uses their forms to give significance to his own feelings.) I have called it metaphysical fear; it would be still more exact to call it unconscious fear, but then 'fear' is no longer an appropriate word. We now know that the primary source of creative activity is a demonic force that is pent in the unconscious, and that this force, when it is released, can assume significance, universal meaning, as a work of art. The more direct this transformation is, the more vital will be the work of art; but such directness is possible only when these demonic forces enter an archetypal form. Such archetypal forms are the characteristic forms of prehistoric art (the bisons of Altamira, for example, or the 'Venuses' of Lespugue or Laussel); but they recur throughout the history of art, wherever there is a *participation mystique* with the demonic forces of the unconscious, and where the artist, with the unparalleled power of a Vulcan, can contain these forces and forge them into symbolic icons.

Since he was awarded the International Prize for Sculpture at the Venice Biennale in 1956, Lynn Chadwick has developed his individual style in a perfectly consistent manner. There have been no radical changes either of subject-matter or of aesthetic purpose. He is still preoccupied with states of attention or alertness in the human figure or the animal. His aim is to incorporate a moment of maximum intensity, and this he does by the most direct means – the reduction of bodily attitudes to their magnetic lines of force.

On what distant point do these lines of force converge? What outer pole of attraction reduces these forms to their corporal economy?

There are three main archetypes: the tensed animal, the stranger flexed for flight, the watcher.

The animal is tensed by fear of the unknown; the stranger has come from the unknown and is ready to depart for the unknown; the watcher waits for the unknown.

The modern artist is alerted to the unknown. Life in its diurnality, its normality, its banality, no longer interests him, or no longer inspires him. Modern man in general is bored with the known, and

all his energies, intellectual and intuitive, are pro-
jected into regions as yet unknown – the unknown
universe, the unknown psyche. In outer space, Yuri
Gagarin tells us, the earth is a delicate blue ball,
floating in black space. This is a new vision, a new
sensation. Lynn Chadwick's vision has penetrated
a psychic region where man is a tensed geometrical
aeronaut, watching the skies, wings folded or out-
spread for flight. Such is the new image of man,
the archetype of a space age. Even his animals look
outward, as if baying at the moon.

But a new vision, not a gadget. Medieval man
had a vision of angels and archangels. On the abyss
of the five senses William Blake saw a mighty devil
folded in black clouds. To such legendary fancies
the artist gives visible shape. But the modern artist
must create his own legends; he is like the modern
child who no longer believes in fairy tales and is
driven by his subliminal needs to invest toy machines with magic. The artist has more liberty than
the child or, what really constitutes liberty, more
creative power. He can give substance to his
apprehensions, to his anxiety. The unknown remains unknown, but this is the moment before a
revelation, the moment of waiting and watching.

> There is the process of metal in me;
> the hardening of the light that gives
> the lucent glory to the eye . . .
> the dark clatter of gears and the mechanical

clicks of the tissue of fury.
I've watched Dionysus step like a scimitar
through my side.*

The great sculptors of our time—and this is an age of great sculpture—are distinguished from most of their predecessors by their sense of the numinous. The early sculptors of Sumer, Assur, Mexico had such a sense; the mask-carvers of Africa and Oceania had it. It is the sense of an incorporated life-force, of a stream of vital consciousness that fuses the matter (stone, bronze, steel) into sensuous and significant shapes: the artist being the welding instrument, the directing channel of a super-human energy. Lynn Chadwick has recovered and reified this vital force, this 'tissue of fury'.

* Ned O'Gorman: 'Two Poems on the Creation of a Statue of a Maenad', *Adam before his Mirror*, New York, 1961.

# PAUL DELVAUX

PAUL DELVAUX is no longer young – he was born at Antheit-lez-Huy in 1897. In his maturity he has developed a style which is completely original and which is of considerable significance for the future of painting. Before such a bold statement can be justified it will be necessary to consider for a moment the relative importance of imagination and technique in the history of modern painting.

It is obviously true that technical considerations have played an enormous part in the actual evolution of modern painting, and since these technical considerations could always be examined in an objective spirit, the science of art criticism, such as it has been elaborated by writers like Morelli, Wölfflin, Berenson and Roger Fry, is largely occupied with the analysis of style and composition. The *obvious* difference between the painting of Giotto and his Byzantine predecessors was a difference in freedom of composition and naturalism of effect; the *obvious* difference between Giotto and Masaccio is of the same kind – still greater freedom, still more naturalism of effect. From that point onwards painting seems to be a progressively successful attempt to solve the problem of representing space and volumes, until perfection is reached in the art of Raphael. But even then, having solved as it were the simple problem, painters began to set themselves special problems, to invent new difficulties to be overcome. The landscape, which presents so many problems of recession and atmosphere, is separated off from the hitherto indispensable human subject-matter and becomes an end in itself. Still-life, a further step in de-humanization, becomes the supreme test of a painter's skill, and the way is open to a process of development which ended in our own time in cubism and abstract art.

But it is possible to look at the history of modern painting from a very different point of view. Giotto represented, not only a technical revolution, but also an imaginative one. He broke away not only from the formal composition and hieratic style of medieval painting, but also from its intellectual symbolism. The freedom he introduced was not only a freedom of style, but also of subject. He humanized the treatment of religious subjects, tried to invest them with an atmosphere of con-temporary reality – tried, that is to say, to imagine them as they *might* have happened. Then, in the course of time, as the imagination expanded in its new freedom, art sought for new inspiration and found it in the pagan culture of antiquity. There occurred that tremendous expansion of curiosity which we call the Revival of Learning, and painters were free, not merely to treat religious subjects in a humanistic spirit, but to desert religion altogether and find their inspiration in the Greek and Latin classics. In this new field there was not the shadow of a tradition to bind them; there were, indeed, fragments of ancient sculpture and perhaps even of ancient painting which were eagerly sought after and studied. But in the main, when it came to giving a plastic interpretation of the mythology of Greece and Rome, there existed no more than a few lines of Ovid to touch off their visual imagination.

When, in the course of the seventeenth century, this immense impetus began to peter out, then technical considerations began to predominate in the painter's mind. The old themes are repeated, endlessly, but it is now a question of the *how* rather than of the *what*; academies are instituted to teach the how, to stabilize it and patent an official brand of perfection. There were to be brave attempts to recover imaginative freedom – the bravest was Delacroix's – but with the Impressionists painting sank deeply into a technical rut; from which it was rescued by the painters of our own time.

There is one dilemma which the technical school of criticism never faced – perhaps was never aware of. According to their scale of values, the difference between Giotto, Masaccio, Leonardo and Raphael is a qualitative difference. If Raphael is acknowledged as the zenith of perfection and represented by the figure 100, then it should be possible to assign approximate percentages of perfection to other painters. Giotto might be 40, Masaccio 50, Perugino 80, and so on. In such a scale of values it would be difficult to give a painter like Bronzino a very low place – it might be 70. But none of the critics I have in mind would like to admit that Bronzino was a greater painter than Giotto or Masaccio. I am not suggesting that technical criticism is valueless; it is extremely important for purposes of identification and classification. But I do assert that the real basis of appreciation, even with the majority of such critics, has little or nothing to do with technical considerations. There may be many factors involved in any particular case, but broadly speaking the qualities that engage us in pictorial art (as in poetic art) are imaginative.

It is a dim realization of this truth which is at the bottom of the present crisis in contemporary art. If once the technical problems of painting and sculpture are relegated to a subordinate position, and imaginative values are allowed to triumph, we shall have to revise our critical standards to meet a complete revolution. The revolution is already far advanced. From such a broad point of view the surrealist movement is to be seen as an emergence from the technical cul-de-sac of Cézanne (a painter who renounced the imagination)*. And it is a new

* ' . . . we must render the image of what we see, forgetting everything that existed before us'. Letter 23 October, 1905.

mythology, a new subject-matter, which the surrealists are seeking. The only substitute for a Revival of Learning provided by the modern age is the discovery of the unconscious. The only modern substitute for the myth is the dream.

The special virtue of Delvaux, as distinguished from a more typical surrealist like Dali, is that he has given what I would call a poetic coherence to his dream world. His myths are viable; they can take root in our conscious life. I am not for a moment questioning the necessity, still less the actuality, of Dali's wonderful and terrifying inventions; but I believe that the word 'invention', which I have used without deliberation to describe them, is more accurate than imagination. Dali, it has always seemed to me, moves rather coldly and logically among his symbols; Delvaux is sensuous and instinctive.

There is, alas, no modern Ovid; but if there were, a painting like *The Call of the Night* would be his plastic equivalent. If we compare such a picture with its Ovidian equivalent – with, say, Piero di Cosimo's *Death of Procris* in the National Gallery – we shall be relatively at a loss. In the case of Piero's picture we have a field of reference, however vague – our knowledge of Ovid or the legend of Cephalus and Procris. I believe Delvaux has an even more valid field of reference – a field which Freud has explored and in which we all walk blindly.

## RUTH FRANCKEN

RUTH FRANCKEN seizes the intangible opposi-
tions of our emotional life – love and hate,
male and female, light and shadow, hope and despair, pride and submission – and from their chaotic
conflict creates symbols of unity and integration.
Her imagination is a heraclitean fire in which
many irreconcilable elements are smelted into the
*aurum aurae* of art. Each painting is an opus achieved
by a magical process of transformation: the formula
a secret which even the artist cannot reveal.

Fifty years ago Kandinsky guessed that the art
of the future would be an 'art of internal necessity'.
But he also realized, so long ago, that a spontaneous
expression of internal necessity is not enough: there
must supervene a further process of 'composition'.

Much of the art of the present moment can be
adequately described as improvisation. Painters
find virtue in the fact that no element of conscious
purpose comes between a paroxysmic action, brush
in hand, and the *tabula rasa* of the canvas. Their
paintings are like signatures, habitual gestures.
They have 'style', and the style is without doubt
the man himself!

But a work of art must have 'form' as well as
'style', and in that fact is the difference between

improvisation and composition. Between style and form there is an abyss, which must be leapt, not crossed by bridges.

The difficulty is to avoid the intervention of a cold calculating spirit that turns improvisation into an academic exercise. Form as well as style must be spontaneous. 'Ses œuvres', said Baudelaire of Delacroix, 'sont des poèmes, et de grands poèmes naïvement conçus exécutés avec l'insolence accoutumée du génie'. *Naïvement conçus* – in this fact lies the difference between works of genius and works of talent.

Spontaneous form seems to be a contradiction in terms. We associate spontaneity with instinct, with an internal necessity; form with the intellect, with conscious calculation.

Nevertheless, even the unconscious is not without intimations of form. Jung has called them archetypes – innate 'axes of reference' round which the incohate substance of the mind crystallizes into definite and significant forms, forms of social significance. If the artist could project such forms, they would be symbols claiming our allegiance, however obscure their meaning.

A few contemporary painters seem to be striving to project from the unconscious the inwardly gestated, preconsciously formed, symbolic archetypes. Ruth Francken is one of them. She has proliferated a world of forms that are not calculated, that are above all *naïvement conçus*, and of great potency. From a frail spiritual furnace, which on the surface burns so calmly, emerge metallic Behemoths and writhing Leviathans, all the more potent for not yet being encased in the carapaces of conventional myth, shimmering, still liquescent in the flames of the imagination. The labyrinth of the psyche was never trod so fearlessly, nor its secret denizens more successfully led quivering to the sunlit surface.

Her paintings are nets in which an eagle or fiery dragon is caught and lies subdued, wings crushed against the silken strings; waxen cells from which a golden chrysalis emerges with scales of fearful symmetry; magnetic fields in whose furrows the wandering atoms reveal their secret lines of force; voids in which the invisible ether coagulates to give birth to a microcosmos. The consciousness of the artist is a clear integument, stretched taut in a passionate effort of apprehension, on which a transcendental reality slowly crystallizes like frost on a window-pane. The unknown is feared unless it can be thus delineated –all profound art is a process of establishment and we grow confident and advance to the degree that we are guided by such charts of the *terra incognita* of the psyche.

I have called it an art of potencies, but it is also aesthetically sensitive: potent in form, sensitive in style. I will not describe the methods by means of which Ruth Francken *arrache les entrailles* from the psyche. Sufficient to say that it is a process of attending to the unintended: of patient but unexpectant exploration – a slow *éclosion* in which the details emerge magically from their matrix, until the archetype gleams into the consciousness like a star at dusk.

*Ruth Francken  L'Ardent or The Self-Consumator  1958*

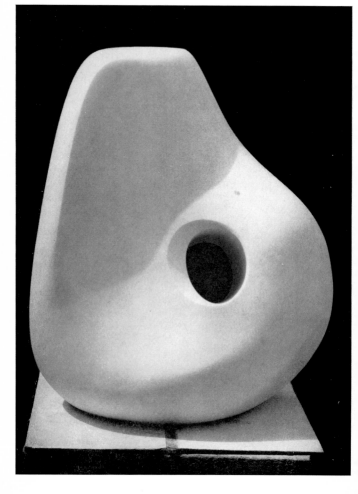

*Barbara Hepworth  Talisman II  1960*

*Constantin Brancusi  The Beginning of the World  1924*

*Sam Francis  Summer No. I 1957*

## SAM FRANCIS

ABSTRACT PAINTING is like music in that it invites subjective reveries rather than precise interpretation. The introductions which critics write to catalogues become like old-fashioned programme notes, but instead of discovering bird-songs and bleating lambs in a Pastoral Symphony, in such paintings we fancy we find archetypes of the unconscious. It is a game anybody can play who has a command of the jargon, but it will not do for the paintings of Sam Francis. They are singularly evasive. They do not readily congeal into images. They usually present a cloud-like and expansive surface that in visual terms say *nothing*, and the mind, always anxious for physical support, glances aside. Nothing, or rather, Nothingness is something that can be said: something to be represented as a metaphysical value, and to be represented physically, aesthetically, as a feeling-value. But that already begins to sound like the jargon I would like to avoid in this note.

It would be much easier to talk about the paint – the *matière* that is so competently displayed, so sensuously exploited. But the physical aspect of Sam Francis's canvases should be obvious to anyone, and it can be analysed no more significantly than the tones of a melody, or the bouquet of a wine. That Sam Francis is a master of line and of colour is very obvious from his watercolour sketches – always exact registers of an artist's sensibility. It should be no less obvious that the same sensibility is transferred to the canvas when he paints in oils. But with what purpose does this artist paint? It will satisfy no one to say that he is trying to touch the intangible, see the invisible, grasp the Encompassing. But that, if I do not misinterpret him, is his highly original aim. I once compared Sam Francis to Shelley – 'the shapes that haunt thought's wildernesses', 'the cloudy strife of Life and Death' – the pictures evoke the poems, but Sam Francis is not romantic. He has much more in common with philosophers like Heidegger and Jaspers – he is one kind of Existentialist, but you will not find him in a bistro. He is highly conscious of the incompleteness of man's vision and consciousness, and he seems to be striving to grasp just this – another dimension of awareness.

I am guessing, of course – just as the writer of musical programme notes guesses. Sam Francis has not, so far as I know, given us a clue – the kind of clue that Brancusi, or Braque, or indeed most artists will sometimes concentrate in an epigram. To call an artist a mystic is not very helpful, unless like Fra Angelico he has a religious vocation. And yet I am above all impressed by the seriousness, even the solemnity, of these paintings. Sam Francis must not be confused with those 'action-painters' who hope to achieve greatness by riding their brushes as if they were witches' brooms. He is, on the contrary, a very deliberate, a highly conscious and conscientious painter. There is not a nuance in his paintings that cannot be intellectually justified. I am not speaking of the analytical intellect, but of the visionary intellect – the illuminating intellect that pervades the *Paradiso*:

> E vidi lume in forma di riviera
> Fulvido di fulgore, intra due rive
> Dipinte di mirabil primavera . . .

There are many lines in the *Paradiso* for which Sam Francis's paintings might be the illustrations.

## TO BARBARA HEPWORTH

WHEN I HEARD that Dr Lejwa wanted me to write an introduction to your catalogue, my first instinct was to refuse – just because I have written so many such introductions, and the convention becomes a little stale. Especially in your case, I felt I could not once again offer my inadequate words as a buffer between the uninitiated visitor to the exhibition and the works themselves, in all their plastic innocence. I began a letter to you to make my excuses, and in writing the letter I found I had something to say, and that I was saying it in an unconventional way. And so the letter became this introduction.

It is more than a quarter of a century since you found me a neighbouring studio in Hampstead, where a group that included Henry Moore, Ben Nicholson and Paul Nash, worked in close proximity until dispersed by the outbreak of war. The beginning of that experience is recorded in *Unit One*, the book we published together in 1934. When I turn the pages of this book nowadays I am overcome with nostalgia: how young we were (though we had all reached our thirties) and how full of hope and energy. We had the will to make a revolution, and now we can look back on this quarter of a century

and say that we have made it – made it in spite of the
interruptions of war, in spite of political disillusion-
ment, in spite of the heartbreaking indifference of
the British public. (We won our victories in Venice
and São Paulo, in New York and Tokyo, and even
in the fortress of Paris – only when our artists came
home with their trophies did their reluctant
countrymen begin to acknowledge their merit.)
Looking back to those statements we made in 1934
I can see that we came through because we had
something more than energy and ambition: we had
a vision – a universal or abstract vision of beauty, as
you called it, to which we devoted our lives without
any thought of immediate profit or fame. Do you
remember what you said in that statement of 1934?
– it bears repetition:

'The predisposition to carve is not enough, there
must be a positive living and moving towards an
ideal. The understanding of form and colour in the
abstract is an essential of carving or painting; but it
is not simply the desire to avoid naturalism in the
carving that leads to an abstract work. I feel that
the conception itself, the quality of thought that is
embodied, must be abstract – an impersonal vision
individualized in the particular medium.'

What we have called 'abstraction' in Art has
always been more than a technical conception. Art,
as indeed all life, is a combination of spirit and
matter, and though we may hesitate to define spirit,
we know that it exists, and that it is a subtle

essence that flows only into vessels of grace. It is present in nature, it is present in the human figure; but it is not present in our imitations of these things unless the matter has been re-created. We cannot design beauty, we cannot manufacture beauty; we can only give it birth, by a process that is analogous to the biological process of conception, prolonged gestation, and delivery in travail. To watch the gradual emergence of the figure from the block of stone is to watch the spirit in-forming the matter, fusing the intractable substance to organic shape and vital rhythm. How can such a process be confined to imitation? Must it not rather seek a perfection of form that is a harmony of spirit?

That, in my observation, has been your constant search. The only difference, as compared with the past, has been your different conception of harmony. In the past harmony was conceived as a relationship we derived from nature – the Golden Section was reduced to a mathematical equation (a modulor, as we now call it) and painters, sculptors and architects were taught to use this equation much as a tailor uses his measurements to make a suit. But harmony cannot be created by measurement or by the exact imitation of harmonious objects in nature: it can only be communicated by the flow of spirit into matter. I am not trying to obscure the process in mystical language: it is a practical process, as all creative artists know. The wood-worker in Chuang-Tzu gives the simple explanation.

He had been carving wood into a stand for hanging bells or musical instruments, and when he had finished the work was so perfect that onlookers thought there must be a supernatural explanation. But the wood-carver explained it in this way: 'I am a simple craftsman and have no special powers. But when I am ready to make such a stand, I try not to waste my spirit. I fast in order to reduce my mind to a state of serenity. After three days in this condition I no longer expect any reward or official recognition for my work. After five days I am indifferent to praise of any kind for my work. After seven days I become unconscious of my body and my four limbs. Then, with no thought of the Court present in my mind, my skill becomes concentrated. I go to some mountain forest and select a suitable tree which I know will contain the form that harmonizes with my inner nature. I can now see the bell-stand in the tree and then, but not till then, I set to work. I bring my own natural capacity into relation with the nature of the wood. The heaven in Nature unites with the heaven in Man.'

I doubt if you had ever read this parable of Chuang-Tzu's in 1934, but your words then were almost the same as the words of the Chinese wood-carver: 'It is the relationship and the mystery that makes such loveliness and I want to project my feeling about it into sculpture – not words, not paint nor sound; because it cannot be a complete thought unless it could have been done in no other

way, in no other material or any different size.
'It must be stone shape and no other shape.'

That is the process (subtle but not supernatural)
that I have been watching all these years; that I have
watched with increasing wonder and admiration.
Your achievement is now secure, and though no
artist will ever admit that his work is complete
(for creation, in an artist's life, is a vital function),
nevertheless, as your exhibition will show, there is a
sense of fulfilment in your work, you have found
the Hesperides. I am quoting too much, but there
is a poem of Lawrence's that comes to my mind at
this moment, and since it too uses the image
of the carver, I will end this letter with its appropriate words:

Not I, not I, but the wind that blows through
me!
A fine wind is blowing the new direction of
Time.
If only I let it bear me, carry me, if only it
carry me!
If only I am sensitive, subtle, oh, delicate, a
winged gift!
If only, most lovely of all, I yield myself and
am borrowed
By the fine, fine wind that takes its course
through the chaos of the world
Like a fine, an exquisite chisel, a wedge-blade
inserted;

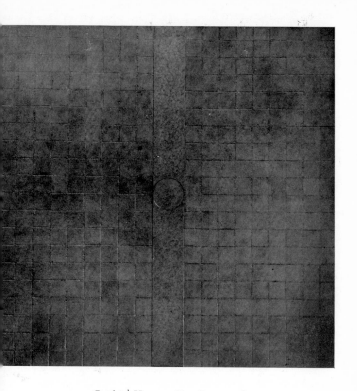

*Gottfried Honegger   Meta Rouge   1961*

*Paul Klee Paukenspieler 1940*

If only I am keen and hard like the sheer tip
    of a wedge
Driven by invisible blows,
The rock will split, we shall come at the
    wonder, we shall find the Hesperides.

Your exquisite chisel, dear Barbara, has come at
this wonder, and I for my part 'would blur no
whisper, spoil no expression' of its pure revelation.

## GOTTFRIED HONEGGER

HE IS AN ARTIST of great *sagesse* – a 'knowing one', as we say in England. His pictures are the result of calculation, but of calculation as Kandinsky defined it, a calculation in which there is no element of rationality, but only feeling or intuition.

His pictures are built up, tessera by tessera, like the mosaics of Istanbul or Ravenna, but with subtle delicacy. The result is at the opposite extreme to *l'art informel*: there are no gestures, no calligraphy – in the normal sense, no expression. The personality, as an ectoplasmic excretion, is excluded, or hidden behind the glowing *vitrail*, in which, nevertheless, there is life – life-blood, one might say, since red is the artist's favourite colour.

Observe the *facture*, which is not a geometrical design, but a revêtement of carefully calculated variations, small gradations of level, plane and direction which together constitute a unit of sensibility. Again the medieval analogy is suggested, for similar irregularities occur in mosaics and stained glass windows. But the unity is as important as the variety.

The result is an icon which we can contemplate – this is, indeed, an art of contemplation. A work of art, according to Simone Weil's definition, is something we can contemplate – not merely glance at, as we glance at a signature, but live with, in stillness and ecstasy, worship.

The principle of composition is one which is also common to music and poetry: to organize sensations in harmonic progression. The visual image in this respect is an object no less real (no less magical) than a word or a note: it has precise shape and outline, and the sensuous overtones come from the calculated intervals (of space) and the varied intensities (of colour). The progress is in time: the structure in space.

*L'art informel* is *un art sans durée* – spontaneous, instantaneous. It has the virtues of immediacy. The art of Honegger is an art constructed in time, and for time. Time, infinite time, is of its essence. Space, too, of course: there can be no plastic reality without space. But the forms, in these icons, move in and through infinite space, and the act of contemplation which they invite becomes a meditation on the mystery of time and space, the mystery of *Dasein*, of the Being that awaits the revelation of the recording artist.

# PAUL KLEE

KLEE HAS SOMETIMES been depreciated in the past, partly because outside Germany and Switzerland his work was little known; partly on grounds of scale and method; and naturally for his tendency, which has been variously described as illustrative, literary, playful or mystical.

No modern artist's reputation has advanced so rapidly since the war – this is shown, not only by the number of appreciative books and articles that have been written about him, but also by the zeal with which his pictures are now collected all over the world. Even Paris, that resisted him for so long, has surrendered to his appeal. Picasso visited him in 1937, three years before Klee's death, and summed up his impression of the artist in the cryptic phrase 'Pascal-Napoleon'. 'Presumably', Will Grohmann has suggested 'he recalled the strange mixture of wisdom and excessive energy, of passionate asceticism and directed intensity, as well as the trace of a Mediterranean origin in his appearance.'*

The complaints about the scale and methods of Klee's painting are now seen to be irrelevant. Klee was an illuminator, and in one sense his art is a

* *Paul Klee*, London (Lund Humphries), 1954, p. 93.

revival of the methods of the medieval manu-
script painters, and like their work, must be seen in
series, not as isolated paintings. This method was
perfectly adapted to his aim, which was the piecemeal revelation of an inner or subjective world of
experience – what Werner Haftmann* has called 'a
morphological process, a process of genesis'. The
name of Goethe may be cited in this connection –
Goethe for whom the world of art was a second
Nature, a spiritual cosmos parallel to the physical
one. 'Art is parallel to creation', wrote Klee in
one of his aphorisms; 'sometimes it is a sample, just
as this earth is a sample of the cosmos.'

The nature of Klee's art is illuminated by the
names of those artists of the past for whom he felt a
special sympathy – first of all, Blake and Goya, and
then Leonardo, Rembrandt, El Greco, Cézanne,
Delaunay and Ensor. Klee was such a various
artist, and yet such a consistent one, that he could
learn from all these masters and yet remain master of
himself. At first sight his relation to Cézanne,
for example, might seem to be rather remote; but
as Dr. Haftmann has shown in a fine page of analysis,
they both had the same conception of a picture as
'an independent organism that had to be complete
within the rectangle of its frame' – Cézanne's *motif*.
Klee's debt to Delaunay was more technical – a
solution of problems relating to light and colour –

* *The Mind and Work of Paul Klee*, London (Faber & Faber),
1954.

131

'how all-pervading light suggests rhythms which obey simultaneous colour contrasts, how object and form are built up of light and colour, rhythmic in appearance, poetic in feeling' (Grohmann). Blake's affinity is the nearest to the essential Klee, but it is doubtful if he had any close acquaintance with Blake's graphic work, and his own development was to be in quite a different direction. But that direction was just as mystical as Blake's, though the mysticism of the one is Christian and transcendental, of the other pantheistic and elemental. 'All art', Klee said, 'is a memory of age-old things, dark things, whose fragments live on in the artist.' Like Rilke, he was much preoccupied towards the end with the angel-image: but his angels were not denizens of a heaven, but beings intermediate between life and death, between the visible and the invisible, 'transitions and symbols of the last mutation, creatures neither "terrible" nor "deadly in their majesty" '.

Klee's pedagogical writings, now conveniently assembled in one volume,* have sometimes been compared to Leonardo's Notebooks. Leonardo, of course, covered a much wider and more confused field of knowledge: in general Klee keeps to the one subject, a theory of the origins and significance of pictorial form. Being also a man of wide general

* *The thinking eye.* The Notebooks of Paul Klee. Edited by Jürg Spiller. London (Lund Humphries) and New York (Winterbottom), 1961.

culture, there is evidence on almost every page of his philosophical background and of more than one kind of aesthetic experience – as is well-known, he was a musician of great talent, and a poet in his vivid command of image and metaphor. His understanding of the physical sciences was also exceptional.

Klee realized that in order to understand the nature and significance of the activity we call art, we have to go back to the origins of the world we live in and try to reconstitute an 'infinite natural history' that traces the emergence of a cosmos from chaos. Form, or rather the genesis of forms, is the basic principle of the universe, and all that constitutes significance, to our human understanding, is either a natural or an artificial *order* won from this chaos. Natural order is organic, the balance of opposites achieved in growth, biological equilibrium; artificial order is geometric, measured or measurable, intellectual. Such polarities penetrate the whole of existence: a concept is not thinkable without its opposite. Beginning in this way, Klee is able to build up a complete morphology of nature which then, at the critical point, has merely to be inverted or transformed to constitute a morphology of art. But 'what we are after is not form but function'. A machine functions, and the universe has often been conceived as a machine. 'But Life's way is something more. Life engenders and bears.' Art, too, is more than a functional activity. We say that it is 'creative'; its forms are 'living'. Here is the mystery to be investigated.

Klee was quite convinced on one point which the apologists for modern art sometimes forget: 'the artist is a man, himself nature and a part of nature in natural space.' 'For the artist, dialogue with nature remains a *conditio sine qua non*.' This led him, in his pedagogics, to a thorough investigation of natural forms, and his final metaphor for the artistic process is that of the tree – he calls it a 'parable.' The artist has his roots in the things of nature and of life, and from these roots the sap rises through the trunk, which is the body of the artist, and then unfolds in space and time as the crown of the tree. We do not expect the crown of the tree to be the mirror-image of the roots, so all art is a transformation of reality and experience. The artist is the channel for this process of transformation, a humble go-between, who should not identify himself with the crown of the tree.

Klee does not remain satisfied with metaphors. He proceeds to a formal analysis of the work of art more penetrating and exact than any ever made before in aesthetics. Some of it is perhaps a little obvious, but completeness is essential to Klee's purpose, which is to show how form comes into being, how structure is achieved, how spatio-plastic elements acquire their stylistic and figurative significance and colours their infinite reverberations.

'Art does not reproduce the visible but makes

visible'. This sentence, which opens the 'Creative Credo' Klee wrote in 1920, is not only an aphorism that concentrates in a few words the precise aim and distinctive character of the modern movement in art; it is also an affirmation, very necessary in our time, of the vital necessity of what Goethe called 'an exact sensuous imagination'.

## LOUIS LE BROCQUY

THIS PAINTER from Joyce's Dublin did seem when I first met him in 1944 to have some qualities of Celtic origin. His images might have been found in a crock of gold, and both Yeats the poet and his brother the painter might have been among his ancestors. But since then Le Brocquy's art has become emancipated from provincial myth and is now both independent and universal. He lives in the South of France, but he is a painter of the inner world of feeling, and has become most curiously original. His work (as perhaps all original work) reconciles two opposed principles, which I will tentatively call innocence and experience. The wide areas of pure white seem to be symbols of a purity waiting to be defiled, an innocence to be outraged. And out of the white screen there do gradually emerge images of erotic fervour. Always (in spite of their superficial abstraction) figurative in intention, the images are in fact human and corporeal. The body, usually female, is reduced to a clotted ganglia of blood and nerves, but recorded so discreetly that the full force of the erotic imagery is only revealed to quiet contemplation. When it finally makes its visual impact, it lies there on the *tabula rasa* of a consciousness not cluttered by the clumsy scaffolding that supports the clichés of the average figurative composition. The eroticism is intense, but is suspended in this aureole of immaculate innocence. One might speak of rites of purification, but that would be to impose on Le Brocquy an ethical intention which I am sure is far from his painterly rectitude. An artist plays with opposites, reconciles them in an equilibrium that is aesthetic, not ethical. The process was perfectly described by Donne in *The Extasie*, particularly in these lines:

> As our blood labours to beget
> Spirits, as like soules as it can,
> Because such fingers need to knit
> That subtile knot, which makes us man
> So much pure lovers soules descend
> T'affections, and to faculties,
> Which sense may reach and apprehend
> Else a great Prince in prison lies.

We call Donne a metaphysical poet, but I doubt if Le Brocquy should be called a metaphysical painter. We have another terminology at our command now, thanks to modern psychology. One always hesitates to apply such terminology to a living artist, for fear of exploding repressions from which the artist unconsciously derives his creative energy. But one may hint at analogies. Readers of Melanie Klein will know what I mean by the good object, milk-white and beneficent; they will also know how often, in the psyche, this object is associated with erotic envy, aggression and sadism. And finally ('in the final analysis') this is perhaps a clue to the mysterious significance of Le Brocquy's painting. In any case, there can be no doubt that after many patient years of research this painter has found the irreducible symbols for what is basic to the life of the spirit, those principles we personify as Eros and Thanatos.

Further investigation of this symbolism would be clumsy. It is preferable to remain on the sensuous surface, so lyrical, so lucid and so deft.

# LE CORBUSIER

## ONE

THE UNIVERSAL MAN (*l'uomo universale*) was the creation of a world of small, independent city-states. Our world, which has made an ideal of the universal in government, culture and soft drinks, distrusts the universal man. He offends against our bouregois love of conformity. We cannot tolerate the idea that a great poet should also be a successful insurance tycoon, or that a professor of physics should play the violin like an angel. Great injustice is done to men who do not comply with this single-track notion of genius. Great injustice is done to a universal artist like Le Corbusier.

Universal man, universal artist – it is the same: the concept of universality is active, creative, and a man is not universal unless he is an artist. A man is not a man, in any complete sense of the word, unless he is an artist in some sense of the word, and a universal man is an artist in every sense of the word. Le Corbusier is labelled 'architect', and the world is willing to admit that he is a good man at his job, a man right at the top of the architectural ladder. But he also writes books – books written in a vigorous style that every academician must envy. It is even whispered that he writes poetry – but no, that cannot be true! Maybe he does a little sculpture too – and that he paints is very evident: the results are around you!

I believe that there is a certain unity in genius, and though a genius may be compelled by circumstance to limit himself to one mode of expression, he has the capacity to express himself in several modes. But usually he is frustrated – he finds no opportunity to develop more than one mode of expression. This lack of opportunity will be inhibitive to the degree that the means of expression are distinct – there is more disparity between the materials of poetry and architecture than between the materials of architecture and the plastic arts. In this latter case the materials are intimately related. In their origins sculpture and architecture were one art, and it is possible to argue that both arts have declined from the moment that they became separate arts. Painting, too, was originally an integral part of the building, and a universal artist like Michelangelo was prepared to decorate a building he designed with sculpture and paintings that he himself executed. Le Corbusier makes the same claim, and the church at Ronchamps is an adequate demonstration of this same universal ability.

What are the elements of painting? First a ground-plan, as in architecture. In both arts, this is the basic element of composition, the foundation of beauty. In the second place, a façade. In architecture the façade is erected in space (in sculpture too);

a painting is hung on a wall, or built into a wall, and is then also a façade, a façade facing inwards. So far the two arts are identical. But then, says the suspicious critic, then comes an important difference which disqualifies the architect who would be a painter, or the painter who would be an architect. *La matière, la facture!* (and at this point French becomes the universal language). And by these, and many other evocative words of the same kind, it is implied that each art has its *mystique*, an incommunicable secret that can only be imparted to those who take vows of aesthetic chastity, and spend the rest of their lives in a narrow cell.

If it is implied that an architect has no sensibility for the sensuous qualities of his materials, the critics thereby reveal their own insensibility to the art of architecture. Every stone has its colour and texture, as rich in impasto as any range of painted canvas. Woods are as subtle as silks, and glass is a jewel gleaming with light. Even concrete has its *force brute*. The truth is that architecture has infinitely more scope, for *matière* and *facture*, than any other art; and painting is merely one instrument in its orchestral composition.

So much for generalities; but Le Corbusier's paintings are divorced from architecture, and ask to be judged as canvases on a wall. They will not suffer from such forced and unnatural isolation: they are faithful and consistent expressions of the genius of this universal artist whom we know as Le

Corbusier. They exhibit his genius for planning space, for erecting a façade, for the sensuous handling of rich materials. They also show a capacity for developing a theme – for that orchestration of *motifs* which is another feature common to all the arts. The theme of the grand design – *Les Taureaux* – which he painted between 1952 and 1955 is one that has haunted European civilization since its beginnings: the Minotaur, the archetype of our ambiguous human destiny, of our terror and our deliverance.

## TWO

The most damning indictment that any future civilization will bring against the first half of the twentieth century is that it lacked the courage of its artists, above all, of its architects. It is easy to attribute this disgrace to capitalism and the profit motive, but it lies deeper than that. Moscow and Peking show that same basic timidity. There have been gleams of light in Brazil, but the visual panorama of the whole world is chaotic. Le Corbusier has not been alone in his frustration – the lives of Wright, Mies van der Rohe, Gropius – all illustrate the same fragmentary achievement, the same frustration by human stupidity. That stupidity,

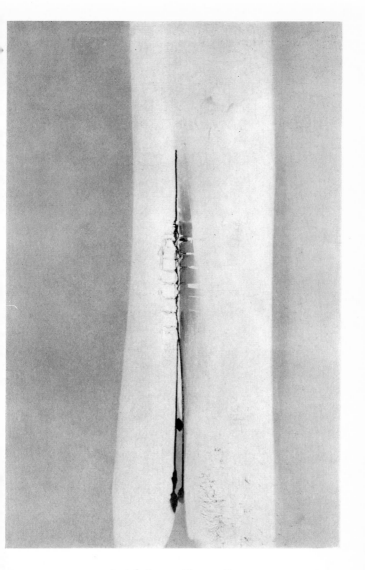

*Louis le Brocquy  Torso  1960*

*Le Corbusier  Painting  1954*

in my opinion, can be defined. It is a rejection of poetry, a masochistic denial of visual delight, and is a product of industrial alienation, a denial of the richness of nature, our own internal nature as well as external nature. 'My research', Le Corbusier declared two years ago, 'is, like my feelings, directed towards what is the principal value in life: the poetry. Poetry is in the heart of man and is the capacity to go into the richness of nature.' How can poetry be restored to life? That has been Le Corbusier's preoccupation for fifty years. He has shown the way. It is for others to follow in that second industrial era 'which will be the era of harmony and is only just beginning.'

## FERNAND LEGER

LEGER IS GENERALLY recognized as one of the great four—the others being Matisse, Picasso and Braque; and though he has none of the variety of the other three, there is a certain integrity or consistency in his work which in the long run may prove to be more enduring. He is also distinguished by a direct and objective relationship to his age which may or may not be of interest to future generations. Picasso and Braque may express the spiritual aspirations of the age (or its nihilism), but the subject-matter of their paintings might belong to any eclectic period. But Léger is an artist of the machine age – even his human figures are mechanized, and he has invented a whole iconography that represents our civilization as effectively as the images of saints represent the Middle Ages. He has not only elaborated the appropriate images, but has also created an appropriate technique of form and colour, and even, as Douglas Cooper has said, *un nouvel espace*. I find it difficult to understand what is meant by new varieties of space, but Léger has certainly carried the use of pure colours to a degree of freedom which almost constitutes a brutal assault on the jaded sensibility of the connoisseur. It is nevertheless perfectly suited to his mechanical images. And it is this brutal quality which has no doubt prevented Léger from developing whole-heartedly into an abstract painter. He has admitted that in his view 'abstract art is dominated by the same desire for complete and absolute freedom and perfection which inspires saints, heroes and madmen' – categories to which he knew he had no pretensions. 'To be free *and yet not to lose touch with reality*' – it is on the horns of that dilemma that Léger has erected his daring art. He does not always succeed; sometimes an image of reality – an eye or a profile – obtrudes with disturbing effect into some otherwise satisfactory abstractions; and sometimes his realism is too blunt and empty. But at his best he is a painter of great sensibility and great power, qualities which do not so readily consort in most contemporary art.

Léger's painting in general raises a problem of some sociological interest. His images are very precise – but representative, not of some vague 'spirit of the age', but of the life and daily pre-occupations of our urban proletariat. During the war of 1914–18 Léger had a revelation of 'the exuberance, the variety, the humour, the perfections of certain types of men' with whom he then found himself in contact. 'I found them poets, inventors of everyday poetic images – I am thinking of their colourful and adaptable use of slang. Once I had got my teeth into that sort of reality I never let go of objects again.' Léger has been, more than any other modern painter, the artist who has given inspired expression to 'everyday poetic images'. But the people from whose ranks he sprang, with whom he has always sympathized, and whose daily life he has depicted, have shown little appreciation of his genius and made no use whatsoever of his capacities. Léger should have been the artist of the great trade unions and syndicates, decorating their halls and factories with his brilliant murals. As a matter of fact the only outlets to this direction of his talent have been given by American million-aires, Swedish ballet producers and the Roman Catholic church. There could not be a better demonstration of the failure of the emergent social forces of our time to grasp the opportunities that have been offered them of creating a concordant culture. Among the major forces of history none has been so visually blind, so aesthetically indiffe-rent, as the one that is now everywhere dominant.

## RENE MAGRITTE

RENE MAGRITTE has dared to take a step which neither Picasso, nor Klee, nor Miró–not even Max Ernst–has yet dared to take. He has dared to assert the self-sufficiency of the poetic idea in painting. I do not mean that he is necessarily indifferent to technique; but technique is only important for the directness and adequacy with which it expresses the imaginative unity of the picture. Visual unity–the sensuous qualities which still intrigue a Picasso or a Miró–these he rejects along with all the babble about form and *facture*. A painting by Magritte is a statement, just as a romanesque fresco or a painting by Van Eyck is a statement: the statement of an idea, a poetic idea. In the case of the medieval artist it is difficult to disengage the poetry from the religion, the idea from the symbol; the modern artist is free to create his own symbols, to exercise the metaphorical activity without restraint. I say 'without restraint', but there is always the restraint that gives unity to the work of art: that cohesion or counterpoise of forces which is the vital suspense isolating the work of art from the chaos of existence. The imaginative process, to be valid, must be logical. Like the logic of reasoning, the logic of imagination has its syllogism, which is an instrument for making judgements or discovering truth. Some day no doubt we shall learn to dissect the imaginative syllogism, but to what end? To distinguish the true from the false? Poetic truth is not in need of such mechanical aids. I possess a beautiful drawing by Magritte. A stream or canal cuts diagonally across a flat landscape; on the right bank, reflected in the water, a curtain – a very bourgeois curtain, hitched up with a girdle – hangs in the sky; on the left bank a tree rises, and its foliage, shaped like one immense leaf, consists of a brick wall; to the left of the tree lies a cannon ball; there is a vague object at the point where the canal meets the distant horizon. It is not difficult to point out a few terms in the syllogism: the straight and horizontal flowing of the canal and the free and vertical flowing of the trunk and branches of the tree; the wide open plain and the hard concentrated sphere of the cannon-ball; the transition from leaves to bricks, both countless, cohering but detachable; tree-wall, wall-tree – it is comparatively easy to reveal this metaphorical activity, just as it is comparatively easy to analyse the iconography of a medieval picture, or the images in one of Shakespeare's sonnets. In that way we project our minds into the picture. But the picture itself is producing a synthesis; its imaginative logic has resulted in a poem, and that poem, unless our senses are dead, we accept in all its compelling unity.

# HENRY MOORE

## ONE

WITHIN A comparatively short time the fame of the English sculptor, Henry Moore, has become world-wide. In Great Britain his importance had been fully recognized as long ago as 1928, when at the age of thirty, he was commissioned to carve one of the four bas-reliefs that decorate the St. James's Underground Station in London. A series of one-man shows in the 1930's won increasing admiration for his work, but then came the war and a temporary check to his activities – it was no longer possible to obtain the stone for his carvings. But Moore's creative energy was not to be suppressed by such material limitations. As a sculptor he had used the medium of drawing for his preliminary studies of a subject, so he began to make many drawings in colour, partly as a record of subjects for future use, but partly also because the medium interested him for its own expressive virtues. Invited to make drawings of war-time subjects, he chose the Dantesque imagery of the underground shelters. In a long series of sketches he gave moving expression to the tragic reality of war as experienced by the ordinary citizen, and this achievement, though a divagation from his main purpose, enormously extended his public.

At the end of the war Moore was invited to hold a retrospective exhibition of his work at the Museum of Modern Art, New York. The exhibition was subsequently shown at Chicago and San Francisco, and everywhere it was admitted that a sculptor of international importance had emerged. The final triumph came in 1948 when the sculptor was invited to show his work at the Biennale in Venice. Moore was awarded the International Prize for Sculpture. After that, even Paris had to admit the existence of an English sculptor. An exhibition of his work was held at the Musée d'Art Moderne in 1949, and was more successful than any comparable exhibition held there in recent times. This exhibition was afterwards shown in Brussels, Amsterdam, Hamburg, Düsseldorf and Berne and from 1950 onwards retrospective exhibitions of Moore's work have circulated throughout the world.

When Henry Moore received the first prize for sculpture at the Venice Biennale there was a general agreement among the world's leading art critics, not only that this artist had become the greatest sculptor of our time, but also that he was an artist whose images were in some manner peculiarly apt to express a consciousness specifically modern in its range and depth. Moore's work must finally be confirmed on grounds that are primarily technical and aesthetic, but that would not be a difficult task: all he has done exhibits the same perfect mastery

*Fernand Léger  Le Soldat à la Pipe  1916*

(above)
Pablo Picasso
Course de Taureaux 1934

Pablo Picasso
Still life with Mandoline and Guitar
1924

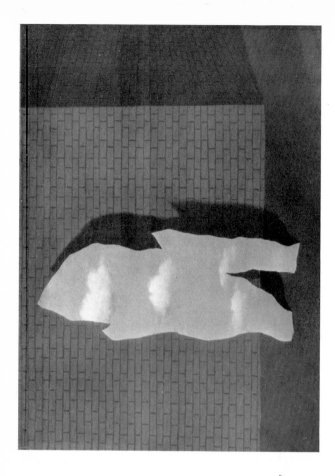

*Réne Magritte*
*L'Epouvantail 1927*

of the plastic values of sculpture – its coherence as mass or volume, its balance and rhythm, the harmonic relationship of part to part, and of each part to the whole. Nevertheless – and this, we may suspect, explains the immediate appeal of his work – these formal elements are always used for an expressive purpose. There is throughout his work a discursive power, an implicit potency, that comes from some deep level of consciousness. His images are archetypal, and are, indeed, confined to a very few archetypes. But this very limitation of Moore's subject-matter indicates a concentration of power reaching deep down into the unconscious, rather than an attention dispersed among superficial phenomena. This strength-by-limitation (character-istic of so many great artists) does not come by conscious choice: it is an imperious and almost impersonal impulse that uses the artist as its medium.

It is not easy to give a brief and simple explana-tion of the qualities in Moore's work that have ensured the universal recognition of his genius. It is partly a question of his integrity. Endowed with a certain feeling for formal relations, he has striven all his life to give expression to this plastic vision. He has taken the most difficult path, working directly in wood, stone or metal, taking care that the forms which he 'discovered' were always forms natural to the chosen material. This led to a characteristic distortion of natural forms, for if flesh is represented in stone it should take on the material and structural nature of stone – it should not be disguised to look like flesh. Sculptors in other ages had established this same 'law', and in this respect Moore is following the tradition of ancient Egyptian, Chinese and Mexican sculptors, as well as the sculpture of the Saxon churches in England itself. But to follow a tradition is not enough. The great artist has in addition a personal 'vision', which is a quality that must be appreciated in front of the work of art itself; it cannot be adequately described in words. It is a question of creating, by abstract means, an impression of vitality. Vitality is, in organic objects, an effect of movement, of growth. The sculptor's problem is to give this dynamic quality to objects which do not move or grow. It is done by creating certain relations between a solid mass and its surrounding space, and by dividing the mass into contrasted areas – convexities and concavities which are rhythmically related and *seem* to move into one another. To create such vitality in an inanimate mass is an infinitely difficult task, and only the greatest sculptors have been capable of it. It demands not only a particular kind of plastic sensibility, but in addition the capacity to translate this sensibility into objective material form.

In modern Europe a sculptor cannot avoid certain humanistic preoccupations. We live in cities, and our whole outlook is anthropocentric. The modern sculptor, therefore, seeks by preference to interpret the human form; at least, this has been the normal tendency of sculpture for many centuries, and in this respect Henry Moore is normal. In his case the tendency has been modified by a desire to relate the human form to certain universal forms found in nature; this aspect of his work I will deal with presently. But first I wish to emphasize the fact that Henry Moore's sculpture is based primarily on the close observation and study of the human form. As a student he drew and modelled from life for many years, and he still periodically returns to life drawing. It is so important to stress this fact, that I would like to quote his own words to me:

'Every few months I stop carving for two or three weeks and draw from life. At one time I used to mix the two, perhaps carving during the day and drawing from a model during the evening. But I found this unsatisfactory—the two activities interfered with each other, for the mental approach to each is different, one being objective and the other subjective. Stone is so different from flesh and blood that one cannot carve directly from life without almost the certainty of ill-treating the material. Drawing and carving are so different that a shape or size or conception which is satisfying as a drawing might be totally wrong realized in stone. Nevertheless, there is a connection between my drawings and my sculpture. Drawing from life keeps one visually fit—perhaps acts like water to a plant—and it lessens the danger of repeating oneself and getting into a formula. It enlarges one's form repertoire, one's form experience. But in my sculpture I do not use my memory or observations of a particular object, but rather whatever comes up from my general fund of knowledge of natural forms.'

That is to say, the artist makes himself so familiar with the ways of nature – particularly the ways of growth – that he can out of the depth and sureness of that knowledge create ideal forms which have all the vital rhythm and structure of natural forms. He can escape from what is incidental in nature, and create what is spiritually necessary and eternal.

But there is just this difficulty: most of the forms of natural growth are evolved in labile materials – flesh and blood, tender wood and sap – and these cannot be translated directly into hard and brittle materials like stone and metal. Henry Moore has therefore sought among the forms of nature for harder and slower types of growth, realizing, that in these he would find the forms natural to his carving materials. He has gone beneath the flesh to the hard structure of bone; he has studied pebbles and rock formations. Pebbles and rocks show nature's way of treating stone – smooth sea-worn pebbles reveal the contours inherent in stones, contours determined by variations in the stuctural cohesion of stone. Stone is not an even mass, and symmetry is foreign to its nature; worn pebbles show the principles of its asymmetrical structure. Rocks show stone torn and hacked by cataclysmic forces, or eroded and polished by wind and rain. They show the jagged rhythms into which a laminated structure breaks; the outlines of hills and mountains are the nervous calligraphy of nature. More significant still are the forms built up out of hard materials, the actual growth in nature of crystals, shells, and bones. Crystals are a key to geometrical proportions assumed naturally by minerals, whilst shells are nature's way of evolving hard hollow forms, and are exact epitomes of harmony and proportion. Bones combine great structural strength with extreme lightness; the result is a natural tenseness of form. In their joints they exhibit the perfect transition of rigid structures from one direction to another. They show the ideal torsions which a rigid structure undergoes in such transitional movements.

Having made these studies of natural form (and always continuing to make them), the sculptor's problem is then to apply them in the interpretation of his mental conceptions. He wishes to express in stone his emotional apprehension of, say, the human figure. To reproduce such a figure directly in stone seems to him a monstrous perversion of stone, and in any case a misrepresentation of the qualities of flesh and blood. Representational figure sculpture can never be anything but a travesty of one material in another – and actually, in most periods, sculptors have tried to disguise the stony nature of their representations by painting or otherwise colouring their statues. It is only in decadent periods that the aim has persisted of trying to represent flesh in naked stone. The aim of a sculptor like Henry Moore is to represent his conceptions in the forms natural to the material he is working in. I have explained how by intensive research he discovers the forms appropriate to his materials. His whole art consists in effecting a credible compromise between these forms and the concepts of his imagination. A similar aim has, I believe, characterized all the great periods of art; the only exception being those rare types of art in which all connection with nature is abandoned in favour of some abstract and disinterested ideal of beauty.

Moore's integrity is not merely artistic: it is also personal. Of simple origins (his father was a miner), he has retained throughout his life a simplicity of manner and a freshness of vision which only those who know him personally can properly experience. But I believe that this quality in the man is transferred to his work. Much modern art can be justly accused of sophistication – sophisticated art being the product of knowledge and imitation rather than of feeling and intuition. I have already admitted that Moore owes his debts to the great masters of the past – no genuine artist would dare to ignore such a treasury of experience. But there is all the difference in the world between the artist who steals from that treasury and the one who adds to it. Moore's sculpture is one of the richest gifts made in modern times to our common stock of enduring art.

Though his work is among the most inventive and experimental of our time, Moore is not a conceited artist—he fully admits his debt to his immediate predecessors and his profound admiration for the great sculptors and painters of the past. The word that most naturally occurs to one in writing about him – and it is a word I have already used – is *integrity*: integrity of spirit and of vision. It is this quality which, transcending the ebb and flow of inspiration, gives to his work its continuing influence and power.

## TWO

For more than thirty years it has been my good fortune to follow with intimate sympathy the unfolding of the genius of Henry Moore. This man was not born with any special privileges. His social origins were lowly and only a strong will and a compelling sense of his own destiny could have carried him through the obstacles that beset an artist in an age committed to the pursuit of material values. Great art has always been the reward for an overcoming of great difficulties, and we may consider lucky a man who is challenged by his fate. Just as the best statues are hewn out of the hardest stone, so the spirit of a great artist is tempered in adversity. Moore came to maturity in the midst of the First World War, but out of this experience (he served at the Front and was wounded) he snatched an opportunity to pursue his studies at a school of art. Once committed to the art of sculpture, he willingly submitted to its discipline. He served long years of apprenticeship with hammer and chisel and stone, and thus acquired a sense of mass and volume, of truth to material and of three-dimensional integrity, which have remained the criteria of all his subsequent work.

Perhaps I give the impression of a ruthless and self-centred egotist, impatient, intolerant and proud; but those are not the characteristics of a great artist, whose strength is always allied to gentleness, whose self-regard is always modest, whose deepest feeling is always humane.

As the years have passed we have seen this artist's work increase by some natural process of procreation, until it now populates a whole world with its forms. How shall we characterize these creatures of his imagination? First, by their *organic vitality*. They are not intellectual abstractions of any kind; they are nervously articulated, and seem to breathe with the spontaneous rhythm of a hidden heart. This is not indeed the only kind of sculpture to which we can give our allegiance – there is another kind that depends on mathematical law, on the intuitive perception of geometric proportion,

*Edouard Pignon  Pleureuse  1946*

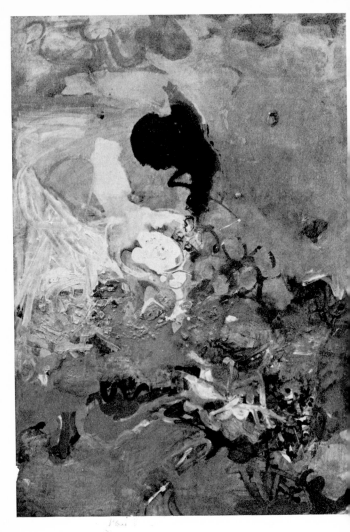

*Paul Reyberolle  Le Couple  1960*

and Moore has occasionally shown that he can be master also of this kind. But in general he has preferred, in the words of Ruskin, to unite the 'implacable severities of mathematics' with 'the softest mysteries of emotion'. As Ruskin observed, only the greatest sculptors have been capable of achieving such a perfect and errorless balance.*

Although Henry Moore has always been an experimental artist, capable of great daring in his formal inventions, yet all his adventures have been guided by a scientific knowledge. He innovates on a foundation of fact. He is familiar with the laws of growth and form, and any strangeness in his proportions is due to his discovery of the secrets of nature. He may assimilate one form to another, see a mountain in a bone, or a deep cave in a human breast; but every feature is organic, and can be referred back to prototypes in the realm of Nature. But he does not, like so many contemporary artists, have recourse to the microscopic world of forms revealed by scientific instruments; he remains faithful to human vision, and for this reason his work retains a sensuousness which is denied to unfamiliar shapes. All Moore's shapes are animistic, haunted by a vital spirit. The spirit may sometimes be imprisoned and tormented, but always it cries out in accents that are human.

To repeat another phrase of Ruskin's, Moore is 'as much master of all the laws of balance and

* The context of this statement is given below, page 231.

weight in the human body as Michael Angelo himself'. But, as Ruskin said of the sculptor he was discussing, Jacopo della Quercia, the sculptor does not wish that you should think of such laws. Perfect knowledge ensures effortless equilibrium. Observe one of Moore's reclining figures. To recline gracefully is in life itself a difficult art for human beings, but in Moore's pieces of sculpture the disposition of the four limbs, the inclination of the torso, the swelling breasts and rounded head, all cohere to form a rhythmical revolution round some imaginary but true centre of gravity. Bosses and hollows, ridges and slopes, move rhythmically in relation to each other – cohere in a linked sequence of modulations. There is nothing violent or abrupt in this world of forms, but there is sometimes an element of terror, of *terribilità*.

This brings me to the most difficult aspect of Moore's work. The modern movement in general has rejected the classical tradition in art. Henry Moore himself has declared, in a well-known statement, that 'beauty in the later Greek or Renaissance sense', is not the aim of his sculpture. But the rejection of beauty does not mean a total rejection of the ideals of art as they have been conceived in the past. Distinct from beauty there was always an ideal of sublimity, and first the author known to us as Longinus, who wrote in the second century, and then in the seventeenth and eighteenth centuries philosophers such as Boileau and Burke, Schiller and Kant, made it clear that there are elements in art, and these of the highest, which have in their nature more of strangeness and terror than of measure and calm. It was Longinus who first suggested that emotional intensity is the mark of the sublime, and this was to be the principle upon which, from the middle of the eighteenth century, and largely on the basis of Burke's interpretation of Longinus, the whole Romantic Movement was to be founded. We are still romantics, however much we may dislike the fact and disown the label, and that 'delightful horror', which for Burke was the true test of the sublime, has never been so evident as in the art of our time, a time in which, as Rilke said:

> das Schöne ist nichts
> Als des schrecklichen Anfang . . .

The present is not the appropriate occasion to discuss such an aesthetic of terror, but Henry Moore has been its greatest representative in our time, and all I wish to emphasize is that in this respect his art should be considered under the rubric of sublimity, not of beauty.

There is perhaps just one other aspect of Moore's work which I should mention, though it is not one of which the artist himself is conscious – I mean its unconscious power. This is but another aspect of its sublimity. By virtue of its intensity and vitality, art of this kind has an ability, which Burke in his *Enquiry* had already observed, 'to pierce into the inmost, and what might appear inaccessible parts of our nature'. Much has been written of the archetypal significance of the images created by Moore, their relationship to the ancient images of the earth goddess, nature goddess or life goddess. There is certainly no deliberate intention on the artist's part to refer us to such archaic symbolism, but Moore's work has always returned to two or three feminine themes, the mother and child and the reclining figure, and there can be little doubt that this obsession has a spiritual significance, and proceeds from the inaccessible parts of Moore's own nature, those parts which merge with the terrors and mysteries of the whole human race.

I have known this artist well, and feel an intimate sympathy for his personality based on our common origins and common aspirations, above all on our sharing of the difficulties of the days before his genius was recognized, when there was much work to be done for little return, and when misunderstanding, bitter opposition and sometimes violent denunciation was our lot. Twenty-seven years ago, when my first appreciation of his work was published,* I already wrote that Moore, like all great artists, was consumed by an endless curiosity – curiosity concerning the possibilities of his materials, curiosity concerning the nature of life; and I already noted, as a matter for wonder in the case of this artist, then only thirty-five years old, 'the consistency of his

* *Henry Moore*, London (Zwemmer), 1934.

course, the gathering power, the increasing clearness of his intention'. The life of an original artist, I concluded, be he painter, sculptor, poet or musician, is hard; 'only an unfailing integrity of purpose can carry him through those years of financial failure, of public neglect and derision which are his inevitable lot. All but a few are compelled to compromise.' But I said then, and can repeat now, that there has been no compromise in the life of Henry Moore; and now, as then, in the fullness of his powers, he offers us the perfected product of his genius.

# PICASSO

PICASSO is a great artist who has survived the test of growing old – he is like a fountain whose waters are inexhaustible. But one can make further use of that image, for he is like one of those illuminated fountains whose colours constantly change. His vitality, his surprising freshness, is perhaps due to the fact that he is master of a dozen media, and of more than a dozen styles. He can switch his enormous spiritual energy from a medium like painting to a medium like sculpture, from engraving to ceramics, and he can express himself in any material whatsoever – in rubbish out of the waste-paper basket if necessary. As for his style, he can be realistic or abstract, impressionistic or expression-istic, as classical as Raphael or as romantic as Delacroix. In the long run this versatility may count against him; integrity of purpose and consistency of style may have a longer survival value, and one has recently heard critics praising Braque for these virtues to the disadvantage of Picasso. But Picasso has been something more, indeed something greater than a painter. He has represented an epoch – an epoch of doubt and disintegration, of war and revolution, of new human aspirations for justice and happiness, and one can think of no one, except perhaps a scientist like Einstein or a statesman like Lenin, who in this respect is so significant. He is a man of our times, at once profound and playful, tragic and inconsequent, destructive and creative, and in all he does and says, all he makes, there is a sense of magic, a prodigious flair, and above all a serious concern for truth, for joy and for beauty.

I have met Picasso only two or three times, so I cannot speak intimately of his personality. But one incident in which I participated is revealing of his temperament and aims. Shortly after the end of the Second World War, I was showing him round an exhibition of children's drawings which the British Council had sent to Paris. He looked at them very slowly and carefully, and at the end he said: 'When I was the age of these children, I painted like Raphael: it took me many years to learn how to paint like these children!'

Picasso was the son of an art master: he grew up in an environment of art and painted from an early age – paintings still survive which he did at the age of fourteen or fifteen which are prodigies of skill. But Picasso grew to realize – and this is the decisive mark of his genius – that skill is not enough – that a great artist must remain a child in the sense that he must see the world innocently, and express himself spontaneously. It is not easy to reconcile these two demands: to be spontaneous is often to release from the unconscious disconcerting nightmares, and these nightmares do not go to pasture willingly with innocent lambs. To make the nightmare lie down with the lamb – that is, so to speak, the magic power given to a great genius, and Picasso possesses this power in abundance.

# EDOUARD PIGNON

VISITORS TO post-war Paris who go there in search of new sensations are apt to return a little disappointed. There is 'Existentialism', but that is a literary and philosophical movement, and though at least one painter has been described to me as an Existentialist (I think it was Tailleux), it is difficult to see in what sense the metaphysics of nihilism can be more characteristic of one modern painter rather than another. In so far as the Existentialist seeks the creation of a concrete material world as the expression of his own personality, and rejects all systems of speculative thought, all structures which remain in the imagination, to that extent he is merely trying to carry over into literature and philosophy the common practice of all modern artists since Cézanne. Existentialism is not the creation of Jean-Paul Sartre: it is a doctrine common to all those who realize that man, deprived of the supports of religion, can only avoid the abyss of despair, of insignificance, of mere nothingness, by his own acts. He must make his own raft to carry him across the stream of time, and that is all he will have to cling to, all his little existence. The projection, the crystallization in material form, of one's self, of one's sensibility, of one's total awareness –

that has been the specific aim of the modern artist, and in this sense Picasso is the greatest Existentialist of us all.

In this sense, too, no artist could be more existentialist than Pignon, who, among a number of French artists who reached maturity during the thirties, seems to be the one who has the firmest and clearest realization of his destiny, and the requisite talent to achieve his aim. He was born in 1905 at Marles-les-Mines in the Pas de Calais, and belongs to the Norman rather than the Latin type of Frenchman. His early teachers were Auclair and Amold, and it is interesting to note that for a time he studied sculpture under Wlerick. These names can mean little to the English reader, but this early phase of Pignon's work shows the strong influence of his social environment, with themes drawn from the miners and workers among whom he lived. A certain political sentiment verging on expression-ism appears in early canvases such as *Le Meeting* (1934) and *Les Révolutionnaires* (1936). But already, in the latter painting, a certain tendency to form-alization is evident, and like the majority of the French painters of his generation, he was gradually drawn into the aesthetic discipline represented by the cubist tradition. Cubism is not, of course, the only tradition in modern painting, and in particular there is that movement towards the liberation of colour represented by the names of Van Gogh, Gauguin and Matisse. For Pignon this element in modern painting was not less important, and the problem was henceforth for him one of effecting a coherent synthesis. At first he attempted to retain a social theme, to paint historical subjects like *The Massacre of the Innocents*, or *genre* subjects like the various versions of *Maternité* (1941). But colour is still keyed down in deference to a certain tonal uniformity. It is only in 1942 (*La table bleue, La table jaune,* etc.) that colour is used in all its primary brilliance, and that the painter becomes liberated from the last bonds of social realism.

To be liberated from the bonds of 'social realism' does not mean that the painter ceases to be a realist: Pignon's compositions continue to be based on an exact analysis of the natural object, but it is precisely this analysis which gives him freedom, for it reveals the structural limits of the object: the skeleton which can be reclothed in vital colours. The exploration continues through a series of still-lifes, in which the human figure, if it appears at all, serves merely as an accessory. But this was a temporary phase: by nature Pignon is profoundly humanist, as his whole development shows, and his recent work is an attempt to carry over into the depiction of the human figure those potentialities of form and colour whose exploration had only been possible in the relatively abstract world of 'still-life'. The result has been the creation of a series of figure compositions that dominate the space in which they are exhibited with all the solemn and hieratic power of a Byzantine mosaic. It is perhaps not a coincidence that this development followed the exhibition in Paris of a series of magnificent reproductions of frescoes from the principal Romanesque churches in France. It is certainly in such frescoes, as in the mosaics of Venice and Ravenna, that we find the historical prototypes for these paintings of Edouard Pignon.

Whether a new 'byzantinism' in art is feasible or not is more than I can say. Hieratic art has always been monumental art – art for display in public places of worship, on ceremonial occasions, parade art. Modern art is bogged in dilettantism, in dealerdom: it is excluded from our buildings by functionalism. The doctrinaires of communism have proclaimed a rigid orthodoxy of vulgar literalism, from which no great art can possibly emerge. Perhaps the French communists, if they ever come to power, will be saved from such stupidity by their native sensibility, and then artists like Pignon, who are not lacking in proletarian credentials, and have too much integrity ever to abandon their principles, will find a social function for their art.

There are those who say that such a reintegration of art and society does not matter – that it is not possible in the present chaotic phase of human history. The only solution of this chaos seems to them to lie in totalitarianism, in dictatorship, in a new academicism. But this is to misunderstand the nature of a tradition or a style in art. 'Le style est l'homme même' – there can be no departure from that truism. No one with a grain of sensibility wishes to forgo the personal element in art: for the artist it is the only reality. What we should seek to re-establish is the social relevance of art. A tradition will follow, because a tradition is merely the continuity established by a society's awareness of its artists. A delicate relationship, no doubt, but a relationship which persists, even when the parties are divorced, as in surrealism. In seeking to be socially relevant, *engagés*, artists like Pignon in France or Henry Moore in England are not in any manner sacrificing their personal integrity or freedom of invention: they are merely trying to create an oasis of reality within the illusion which we call modern civilization. They are also demonstrating that they have no vested interest in the prolongation of a state of chaos.

## PAUL REBEYROLLE

PAUL REBEYROLLE is also a realist, but the rapid evolution of his style from 1957 to 1960 suggests that this label is as meaningless as most labels in the history of art. There is a sensibility – acute, savage, joyful, erotic, harmonious – the epithets are inexhaustible and even contradictory, but nevertheless describe the various facets of a single personality. One grows tired of the battle of styles: the style is the man himself, in his uniqueness, and we each react (if we are capable of reaction at all) as another personality, receptive, but also unique. I know that Rebeyrolle has been claimed for polemical realism – that he has political convictions, and this I respect. But what have political convictions to do with the aesthetic experience? What ideological factor is common to Courbet and Cézanne? Pissarro was an anarchist, a fact which engages my political sympathies, but does not and should not colour my aesthetic response to his work. I do not need to know the politics or the religion of an artist, any more than I need to know the name of his mistress or the address of his colour merchant. Art is a human activity, and always related to the human condition. For this reason, but only for this reason, it has always played a decisive role in the transformation of society. Art is the most powerful of all revolutionary forces (poets the unacknowledged legislators of mankind, as Shelley said). But *unacknowledged*: art works invisibly, silently, by means of images, not ideas. It does not gain its power (it loses its power) by political crudity of any kind: by deliberate brutality, by ideological emphasis. It gains its power from its vision of reality, a vision of the reality that is beyond appearance. Every artist must believe that there exist in the world of the imagination eternal realities of which the work of art is a fleeting reflection – a reflection in what Blake called 'the vegetable glass of Nature'. Rebeyrolle's paintings are reflections of this kind. The reality he seeks is not mundane: it is remote and beautiful, beautiful because remote; it is immediate and vital, vital because immediate. An owl, a frog, a trout; a landscape, a tumbled bed, exhausted lovers: in each subject a synthesis of organic vitality and mathematic beauty. I see each work of Rebeyrolle's as a titanic struggle to achieve such a synthesis. In the past he may have sacrificed beauty to vitality: now he reaches the point of equilibrium, the unmoving centre of our attention. There is still a torment in his compositions: Jacob struggles with the Angel: eroticism with love, time with eternity; but the embrace is locked into stillness, into enduring harmony.

# ANTONIO TAPIES

SOME INDICATION of a painter's intentions can be gained from the titles he gives, or allows to be given, to his works. In the case of Antonio Tapies these are almost always indications of colour only, from which one might conclude that colour is the supreme aesthetic element in his compositions. But we may then note that the colours in question are almost all neutral – many tones of grey, with black, white, and ochre to supply a contrast. In general these colours might be described as earthy, and one is often reminded of the silt at the mouth of a river and of other such natural deposits and accidental effects. Even the graffiti which sometimes score the otherwise smooth surface have the effect of traces left by raindrops or by the scorching breath of the sun. There are two sentences in one of Kipling's stories that remind me of this texture. Kipling is describing a pool of blood drying on a barrack-square in the tropics after a man had been murdered: 'The hot sun had dried it to a dusky goldbeater-skin film, cracked lozenge-wise by the heat; and as the wind rose, each lozenge, rising a little, curled up at the edges as if it were a dumb tongue. Then a heavier gust blew all away down wind in grains of dark-coloured dust.'

*Antonio Tapies  Painting  1956*

*Emilio Vedova*
*Documento I 1957*

The journals of the English poet, Gerard Manley Hopkins, are full of acutely sensitive observations of abstract patterns in eroded matter. He observes in one place that 'it is just the things which produce dead impressions, which the mind, either because you cannot make them out or because they were perceived across other more engrossing thoughts, has made nothing of and brought into no scaping, that force themselves up in this way afterwards'. I am not trying to suggest that Tapies is a naturalistic painter, but his images do not seem to me to be either informal or spasmodic. They are images of actuality, but of an actuality that has not been related to our logical or scientific vision of the world. To risk a comparison in order to be more specific: the images in a painting by Miró have obvious affinities with organic objects that belong to logical vision – the human body, the sun and stars, animals and flowers. Such objects can never be identified in a painting by Tapies, and yet I feel that his images are much more directly related to nature than those of Miró – that this 'black relief with graffiti' or this 'black background with grey and ochre spots' could exist in all its actuality. A 'personnage' in a Miró is a beautiful but grotesque deformation of the natural fact. There is no deformation in a Tapies: his textures are natural, even realistic.

I will risk another comparison. To anyone like myself whose early artistic training was in the art of ceramics, the paintings of Tapies immediately suggest the highly sophisticated beauty of those *raku* wares made in Japan in the sixteenth and seventeenth centuries, rough and unsymmetrical in form with rugged and broken textures of exactly the same colour range. I am not trying to reduce the painting of Tapies to the level of craftsmanship (though what is painting if not a craft?) but I would like to suggest that its appeal is directly sensational. I notice that Michel Tapié has already asserted that Tapies's experiments are 'profundamente pictórica y nada mas', and I agree. I also agree that a psychological approach to his art is out of place (naturally, since art is a psychic activity, all approaches are psychological, but psychological has come to mean 'analytical', and that is the error). The secret of this art is not to be revealed: there is no secret but only a physical object with no more magic than the wind and the rain create in our path, or such beauty as we see when our eyes are not busy constructing a private world, but allow the existing reality to enter the doors of perception unchallenged. What thus exists is invariably beautiful: the difficulty is to have humility of vision.

# EMILIO VEDOVA

V EDOVA'S WORK in its development during the past twenty years illustrates very logically the historical destiny of expressionism. As a style of painting, expressionism began as a revolt against the tyranny of idealism – more particularly, as a revolt against that aspect of idealism known as objective realism, by which was meant the imitation of what is already present in the consciousness as 'nature'. Against this prejudice the artist (aided by pioneers or a new philosophy of art such as Conrad Fiedler and Wilhelm Worringer) dared to assert the legitimacy of the 'free artistic act', the concept of art as the expression of an inner necessity, the belief in the adequacy of form (the *Gestalt*) as a symbol of feeling. Kandinsky in painting and Schönberg in music were the first to break through the last defences of idealism and to establish an art of pure expression, of creative symbolism. In the last fifty years such an art has become a new plastic language, completely independent of the aims and ideals of classical art.

The work of a painter like Vedova shows how slowly and cautiously this new language must be learned. To throw away all the elements with which traditional painting had built up its world of form – the representation of three-dimensional space, the architectonics of mass, the harmonic relationships of colour – one might as well hurl oneself into the sea without knowing how to swim. All the great masters of abstract expressionism – above all its founder, Kandinsky – proceed cautiously from a basis in concrete visual experience. Art is not invention: art is imagination. It always proceeds from the perceptual image, from sensation, from physical experience. On such foundations it can build into infinity – it is a bridge into the spiritual world, as Franz Marc said. A bridge must always spring from solid ground, however high its arches reach. The claims of a pure (immaterial) abstraction are difficult to sustain in any empirical sense: Mondrian's own development is no exception. Vedova's development has been a logical extension of his visual experience, but the farther he has reached towards freedom, towards free expression, the more he has revealed his inner necessities, which are necessities of intolerance, violence, obliteration. It is not for the critic to inquire into the 'inner necessity' which demands such formal conflicts, but they are not confined to this artist – they are within the collective unconscious of our time, our race, and the artist projects them on our behalf: he bears our cross. In such a situation we do not speak of beauty, serenity or pleasure (nor do we speak of such things in the presence of Grünewald's *Cruci-*

*fixion*): we speak of pity, terror and catharsis. Vedova is one of the most tragic artists of our period: it is on the plane of sublimity that we should encounter his work and acknowledge its power of redemption.

Part III

THE AMBIGUOUS ARTIST

# THE ARTIST'S DILEMMA

OUR PROBLEM is to determine what factors in any given period (and more particularly in our own) determine the success of an artist. We cannot begin with the assumption that it is simply a question of genius or talent, for we know that many artists who are later recognized as great artists had no success in their life-time, and that many of those who enjoyed success in their life-time are later forgotten. It is also obvious that the success of an artist in his life-time is sometimes based on qualities different from those for which he is admired by a later age. There is therefore a very complex inter-relationship of several factors, among which it may not be easy to trace the operation of any definite laws – chance may indeed play a great part in a field where so many of the factors are subjective or emotional.

Genius is difficult to define, and we should perhaps confine ourselves to a consideration of the more modest endowment which we call *talent*. The man of genius is always an 'outsider' – what genius does, as Goethe said, is done unconsciously, and the success or unsuccess that attends the work of genius is not the result of the operation of any social laws. A genius is like a comet which for a brief moment flashes across the night sky and disturbs the

normal pattern of the stars; or, to speak less meta-
phorically, genius is a biological 'sport' and not
representative of the species artist.

We cannot exclude unconscious factors from our
discussion, as I shall indicate later; but for the
moment I would like to consider the normal
maturation of a talent, in painting for example, and
ask what qualities in the artist and what conditions
in society make for success. With qualities so
various and conditions so inconstant, any generalization will be difficult.

Let us begin with the artist. We shall assume an
initial endowment, an innate sensibility which at the
approach of adulthood manifests itself in the desire
to be an artist. Here begins the first hazard – the
choice of a profession. It is by no means certain that
the individual in question, on the basis of a diffused
aesthetic sensibility, will hit upon the right craft.
Paul Klee hesitated between painting and music,
and we are glad that he chose painting; but to take
a painter of another age, Benjamin Robert Haydon
(1786–1846); this artist, in the belief that he was
born to be a great historical painter, expended
passionate energy and for a time was able to con-
vince his contemporaries (or some of them) that
he was a great genius; but in the end he failed
miserably and committed suicide. He left behind a
journal which is one of the most interesting docu-
ments in the literature of art, brilliantly written,
and there can be little doubt that if Haydon had

chosen to be a writer instead of a painter, he might have ranked with Scott or Balzac.

Let us assume that the potential artist does not make a mistake of this kind – that he makes the right choice of a craft. The development of his talent will then depend on several factors, the first and most obvious being his physical and mental health. His sensibility is already a reflection of his constitution, and this in its turn is conditioned by hereditary factors and by his early upbringing (again we are directed to the unconscious, for his talent may depend on such factors as the successful sublimation of aggressive instincts, the resolution of the Oedipal situation, integration of the personality, etc.). The will to be an artist emerges from tremendous inner conflicts of this kind, and it is only when all these have been resolved (and it is a problem which involves the individual's relationship to society as a whole as well as to his immediate family environment) only then can he face the still considerable hazards of an artistic career.

The first of such hazards is education – by which I mean education outside the upbringing he receives in his family, public education. This is perhaps the greatest hazard of all, because there is no doubt that most systems of education might have been deliberately designed to stultify the aesthetic sensibility of a child. With rare exceptions public education throughout the world to-day concentrates on the inculcation of intellectual knowledge, for which it requires the development of such faculties as memory, analysis, enumeration, classification and generalization. These are all faculties that either directly deaden or depress the aesthetic sensibility, which needs for its development concreteness, sensational acutenesss, emotional spontaneity, attention, contemplation, wholeness of vision or apprehension, and generally what Keats called 'negative capability'.

The conflict between the intellectual and the aesthetic approach to education was first clearly realized by Schiller and his *Aesthetische Briefe* remain the clearest statement of this inescapable dilemma, a dilemma which is not likely to be resolved by our rationalistic civilization. My own view, which I have expressed in several books, is that the psychic imbalance of prevailing systems of education is directly responsible for the moral delinquency of our populations and their inevitable drift to annihilating wars, but that is a wider aspect of the problem. For the moment I am concerned with the education of the artist, and we may see that the only great artists in our civilization are those who have managed, either by chance or by deliberate effort, to avoid the deleterious effects of conventional education. The public image of the artist is of precisely such a person – the Bohemian, the Outsider – a man who behaves and even dresses differently from 'the man in the street'. In a rationalistic civilization the artist is a pariah.

I have been speaking of normal or public education, but assuming that the would-be artist has
survived this hazard and still persists in his desire
to become an artist, he would then have before him
the prospect of 'art education'. This can be the
worst hazard of all, and a great many talents are
slaughtered in these academic abattoirs. The
conflict between tradition and individual talent
(which is the basic conflict in all forms of social
adjustment) is now narrowed down to the problem
of personal expression, and the would-be artist has
either to accept the academic formulas, which may
extend to style and treatment as well as to more
technical questions of materials and methods of
composition, or to assert his own vision. Success or
failure may depend on the resolution of this conflict.
If the authority of the academy is supreme, as it
was in Europe throughout the seventeenth and
eighteenth centuries, then success depends on the
acceptance and exploitation of the academic formulas. Naturally an unintelligent repetition of these
formulas will not lead to success: the artist must
understand their purpose and may even subtly
modify them to satisfy his personal taste. But to
ignore them altogether is to incur neglect. A good
illustration from the history of English art is
provided by the contrast between the ideals and
fortunes of Sir Joshua Reynolds and his contemporary William Blake. Reynolds was by no
means a narrow-minded pedant; on the contrary,

he was a man of broad sympathies and 'sweet reasonableness', and his own great reputation as a painter, not only in his own time but in the judgement of posterity, makes him an admirable example for the purpose of this discussion. That his success was due to self-imposed limitations – his realization that he had no gift for poetical compositions in the grand manner, but must confine himself to the interpretation of character – only adds to the interest and significance of his case. He has been accused of not practising what he preached (in his *Discourses*), but as Roger Fry pointed out in his edition of the *Discourses* (London, 1905), 'the notion that Reynolds as a critic ought to have bound himself within the limits of his own talent as an artist, that he was to recommend others to do no more than he had done himself, is palpably absurd. It is just because he had the gift, an unusual one among artists, of rising to a general view of art as a whole, and of regarding his own performance with objective impartiality, that he is so remarkable as a critic.'

If we turn to the *Discourses* we find Reynolds recommending that 'an implicit obedience to the *Rules of Art*, as established by the practice of the great Masters, should be exacted from the *young* students. That those models, which have passed through the approbation of ages, should be considered by them as perfect and infallible guides; as subjects for their imitation, not their criticism.'

'I am confident', he adds 'that this is the only efficacious method of making a progress in the Arts; and that he who sets out with doubting, will find life finished before he becomes master of the rudiments. For it may be laid down as a maxim, that he who begins by presuming on his own sense, has ended his studies as soon as he has commenced them. Every opportunity, therefore, should be taken to discountenance that false and vulgar opinion, that rules are the fetters of genius; they are fetters only to men of no genius; as that armour, which upon the strong is an ornament and a defence, upon the weak and misshapen becomes a load, and cripples the body which it was made to protect.'

That Reynolds had the excellence of the art of painting at heart rather than his own social success is not to be doubted, but again and again he points out that 'labour is the only price of *solid fame*', meaning by labour a patient following of the precepts of the Academy, and by solid fame, social success. Nevertheless, towards the end of his *Discourses* he had the generosity to admit that by exception a genius like Gainsborough might arrive at excellence (if not worldly success) in avoiding these precepts – 'he found out a way of his own to accomplish his purpose'. But he warned his listeners against following this example, and in the eloquent conclusion to the *Discourses* he once more affirms that the greatest success in art cannot be obtained by any other means than great labour. Even Michelangelo, who 'might make the greatest pretensions to the efficacy of native genius and inspiration'—even Michelangelo, as he himself said of Raphael, 'did not possess his art from nature, but by long study.'

About 1808, thirty years after they were delivered, Blake wrote some annotations in his copy of the *Discourses* which showed the reaction of native genius to such a man as Reynolds and to his precepts. 'This man', he declared, 'was hired by Satan to depress art,' and Blake had 'nothing but indignation and resentment' to express as he read the discourses of one who had been 'applauded and rewarded by the rich and great. I consider Reynolds's Discourses to the Royal Academy as the simulations of the hypocrite who smiles particularly where he means to betray. His praise of Rafael is like the hysteric smile of revenge. His softness and candour, the hidden trap and the poisoned feast. He praises Michelangelo for qualities which Michelangelo abhorred, and he blames Rafael for the only qualities which Rafael valued' – there is much more vituperation of this kind, about forty pages of it, but apart from a defence of Blake's own style in painting (delineation as against chiaroscuro) they return again and again to two themes: tradition and individual talent, and patronage. Reynolds 'mocked' inspiration and vision ('then and now, and I hope will always remain, my element, my eternal dwelling place'); and he rigged the market in favour of his own kind of art: 'the rich men of

England form themselves into a society to sell and not to buy pictures. The artist who does not throw his contempt on such trading exhibitions, does not know either his own interest or his duty. . . . The inquiry in England is not whether a man has talents and genius, but whether he is passive and polite and a virtuous ass and obedient to noblemen's opinions in art and science. If he is, he is a good man. If not, he must be starved.'

It may seem that this quarrel between Reynolds and Blake is irrelevant to the theory of success in art to-day. It is true that in some countries the academies of the eighteenth century no longer exercise the same degree of power, but they still have prestige among the bourgeoisie, and an artist's election to the academy usually carries with it social and economic success. Success, of course, is an ambiguous concept, and we must always distinguish, as the French do, between *un succès d'estime* and *un succès fou*. But what both Reynolds and Blake are saying is that success is largely dependent on personal qualities – labour in the one case, inspiration in the other. Assuming the possession of innate sensibility, we might conclude that each quality leads to a different kind of success, but unfortunately the artist of solid fame will always envy the inspiration of the native genius, while the native and untutored genius will always envy the solid fame of the artist who has succeeded by the assiduous cultivation of a modest talent.

Another personal factor in achieving success, almost as important as genius or long study, is what we might call charm (though some artists can exploit a reputation for being 'difficult' – anti-charm). This quality is perhaps too obvious to be worth mentioning, but from one's own observation of the world of art one sees what a difference an artist's personality can make. It is not merely an ability to establish easy relationships with his fellow artists, with dealers and collectors, museum directors and critics. All this is more likely to help the second-rate artist than the great artist, who can afford to ignore such refinements (as Michelangelo did, or Gauguin). But since man's character is his destiny, it does follow that the public image of an artist will be formed, not only on the objective evidence of his work, but on the social impact of his behaviour. There is no surer road to success than the creation of a legend: the part played by their romantic, erratic, or merely distressing lives in the success (alas, for the most part posthumous) of artists like Gauguin, Van Gogh, Modigliani, Utrillo, cannot be ignored. But a legend grows: it cannot be deliberately created, though some artists, who lack other means to success, sometimes make the attempt. A legend, we might say, is not created without suffering (*malheur*): very different are those reputations which are the product of skilful publicity. The 'stunt', such as practised in our time so successfully by Salvador Dali and

Georges Mathieu, is art redeemed by the arts of publicity.

The function of publicity must, of course, be taken seriously by the contemporary artist, if only because he is part of an economic system that functions through this medium (the situation is somewhat different in the communist system, but let us exclude this complication for the moment). The life of an artist in the capitalist world must be largely pre-occupied with the problems of exhibition and sale. A very complex sales organization now exists, largely in the hands of private dealers but not excluding artists' societies which are co-operative sales organizations usually for the benefit of artists who have not yet acquired sufficient reputation to attract the interest of a dealer. Sales to collectors do still take place directly, without the intermediary of a dealer; but it is often a condition of the contract between an artist and a dealer that all sales should pass through the dealer's hands – an arrangement that saves the artist a lot of trouble and secures a uniform scale of prices.

Dealers have their own methods of promotion and publicity, and the success of these may determine the success of the artist. There is no exact correspondence between the quality of the art and the success of the artist; as in any other competitive sphere, it is possible to sell an inferior product by superior sales organization – an organization that may extend to every wile of the advertising profession. Works of art are now as subject to skilful promotion as cosmetics or cigarettes. The success that comes from such methods is, however, always subject to independent criticism, and that is why the existence of organs of independent criticism, and of incorruptible critics, is so essential in our time. It should be impossible in questions of taste to fool all the people all the time, but in fact, once an artist has become fashionable by clever methods of publicity, it takes many years of patient criticism to destroy his false reputation – so few people read serious criticism.

The role of fashion, if that can be separated from the methods of publicity, is inexplicable. There are cases of artists who, without any preparatory publicity, and without any claim to greatness, have suddenly become successful overnight. Their works are shown in a gallery for the first time, and without any lead from the critics or any persuasion from publicity, they immediately sell (much more common, of course, is the case of the artist whose work is well received by the critics, well advertised, but completely fails to attract the public). One can only suppose that the artist in this case has by chance satisfied some repressed need in the collective unconscious – there is exactly the same phenomenon in literature, the novel which, for inexplicable reasons, becomes a best-seller.

The element of chance therefore plays a considerable part in the achievement of success – far more than a rational critic like Sir Joshua Reynolds would allow. But this is to consider only happy chances; the phenomenon also has its negative aspects. The lack of success during their life-times of many artists who are posthumously recognized may be due to personal qualities of diffidence, as I have already suggested, or to incompetent methods of salesmanship, but it may be just bad luck. Apart from the bad luck of being born in a remote province, or a small country (chances which afflict the poet much more severely than the painter); apart from the bad luck of being born to poverty or with physical defects (such as bad eyesight), there is an element of fatality in any artist's career which cannot be controlled. In what is at all times a game of chance so much depends upon the people we meet and the places we visit. Many artists have recorded the decisive importance of some strange meeting, of some personal influence that came into their lives with transforming effect. The impact of Masaccio on Fra Angelico is perhaps the typical example. The development of colonialism during the nineteenth century and the consequent importation of an hitherto unknown type of art – the tribal sculpture of Africa and Oceania – is an example from the modern period.

There is one further element which we must now take into account, the most impalpable of all – the *Zeitgeist*. This is a German concept which has been taken over by the rest of the world. Partly it is the question of fashion which I have already dealt with, but fashion is an epiphenomenon, confined to limited circles and of limited duration. The *Zeitgeist* is something that pervades a whole epoch and penetrates all its intellectual manifestations. There is no escaping it, but nevertheless some artists are less subject to its influence than others and these are often the greatest artists. I have already mentioned Blake, and as a poet rather than a visual artist he is as good an example as could be found anywhere. A comparable German poet is Hölderlin, who perhaps had more sympathetic understanding from the carpenter Zimmer with whom he lodged, and certainly from a young student like Waiblinger, than from representatives of the *Zeitgeist* such as Goethe and Schiller. In the plastic arts Hans von Marées is a typical case of an artist who is in advance of his time. Indeed, it is generally true, as Wordsworth said, that an original artist has to create the audience that can appreciate his work. In every successful artist there is a proselytizer.

Finally there is a general sociological problem which is particularly serious in democratic societies and for which, within the general concept of democracy, there is no obvious solution. Success in art, as in any other field of activity, implies distinction, and in a capitalist society it implies relative wealth. It is indeed one of the anomalies of communist society, as it has evolved in Russia and China, that the very concept of artist implies an élite, and artists in these communist societies enjoy, not only a higher status, but privileges of many kinds, not excluding financial ones. It is true that, especially in China, these privileges have to be enjoyed modestly and unobtrusively, but nevertheless they exist.

This problem was recognized by the greatest democratic sociologist of our time, Karl Mannheim. He saw it as a special case of the general problem of reconciling 'freedom' (which the artist needs if he is to function as an artist) with the democratic ideal of 'equality'. In general terms the solution lies in giving art an organic function within the life of the community. Mannheim recognized the dangers implicit in the concept of *art engagé* (socialist realism, propaganda art, etc.) but he thought that the opposite extreme of *l'art pour l'art* was equally dangerous. In the nineteenth century, for example, 'the social position of a large section of the intellectual élite was that of the bohemian, without corporate ties, without a well-defined place in society; the members of this group lived in a curious milieu in which self-styled or genuine men of genius were thrown together with black sheep from aristocratic or bourgeois families, declassé drifters, prostitutes, matinée idols, and other fugitives from organized society. . . . All this exerted a considerable influence upon their thinking. . . . Such intellectuals will cultivate a set of values far removed from the concerns of ordinary people.'

Mannheim was optimistic enough to think that this situation could be changed in a democratic society, not by making the artist a propagandist or a politically conscious individual, but by a process of 'integration', which, however, he does not define in detail. He merely assumes that 'as democratization progresses, the ties between intellectual strata and society at large are likely to become closer and more organic. This need not mean that art will become crudely propagandist, but only that it will have a more organic function in life than *l'art pour l'art* had.'

These words were written in 1933, but the *Demokratisierung des Geistes* to which Mannheim looked forward has nowhere been manifest in the democratic world. Instead art has become more and more abstruse and esoteric, more and more removed from the concerns of ordinary people. To call this development the cult of *l'art pour l'art* does not solve the problem, and is not a scientific diagnosis of a phenomenon now so universal and so spiritually significant as abstract art. One can explain abstract art in sociological terms – as the art of a civilization alienated from nature and from organic processes of production – but this merely means that a democratic industrial society has produced an appropriate type of art. Mannheim indeed recognized that 'there is an intrinsic correlation between the increasing abstractness of the symbols used in communication, and the democratic character of the culture. Elites which are not impelled to make their knowledge generally accessible will not engage in formalization, analysis, and articulation. They will content themselves either with unanalysed intuition, or with sacred knowledge reserved for an élite and handed down among its members *en bloc*.'

The artist in the modern democratic society, Mannheim thought, would gradually surrender his esotericism because in such a society there is a tendency to bar qualitative elements from its experience in favour of greater communicability. But this is not what has happened in the Western World; on the contrary, and in spite of the spread of information through media like television and the film, there is an increasing divorce between art, which increases in concreteness and self-sufficiency, and those media of communication, such as films, television and the press, which communicate through popular images. The result is that there are to-day two distinct criteria of success: the *succès d'estime* which is confined to an élite (albeit an élite of considerable dimensions) and success among the literate masses which is conveyed through quite different media of communication. Necessity of using these ugly neologisms (élite, literate mass, media of communication) is an indication of the unprecedented nature of this cultural situation. Mannheim's hope or belief that these criteria would eventually merge together, that quantitative judgements would coalesce with qualitative judgements in a democratic society, is really a confession that the artistocratic ideals of fine art have no place in an egalitarian democracy. It is a conclusion that was reached, on different grounds, by both Nietzsche and Burckhardt; it is a dilemma that to-day presents us with its naked and unresolved contradictions.

# THE AMBIGUITY OF MODERN

## SCULPTURE

*In a civilization that is rotten with amusement, the more magic we produce the better.* W. G. COLLINGWOOD

SIX YEARS AGO I gave a series of lectures on the Art of Sculpture at the National Gallery of Art in Washington. I returned from America by sea, and shared a cabin with a distinguished sculptor, a Russian by birth, and for many years a friend of mine. He asked if he might see the lectures I had given, so I lent him the typescript which he read for two or three days without comment, but with visible agitation. One day, as he laid aside the last page, he exclaimed: 'If all you say is true, then I am no sculptor!'

Naum Gabo, the sculptor in question, is a Constructivist. With a conceptual equipment unusual in a plastic artist he has, in manifestoes and lectures, given expression to the aesthetic principles upon which his practice is based. These principles do indeed conflict with those which, in my Washington lectures, I had found uniquely characteristic of the art of sculpture as it had been known in the past. Let me very briefly recall those principles, and then consider to what extent they exclude, not only the Constructivists, but also other contemporary schools of sculpture.

In my Washington lectures I tried to isolate and
define a mode of sensibility peculiar to the art of
sculpture, separating it decisively from other arts.
I began by suggesting that distinct modes of sensibility are derived from distinct organs of sensation – in other words, that the arts, and the laws
that govern these arts, would differ according to the
predominance of eye or ear or touch in perception
and sensation. To each particular co-ordination of
the senses corresponds an appropriate art with its
distinct aesthetic laws. 'If we give prominence to
vision and subordinate all other sensation to its law
of maximum aesthetic effect, then we get one kind
of art; if we give prominence to touch and subordinate all other sensations to its law of maximum
effect, then we get another kind of art.' I did not
assume that sculpture is an art of tactile sensation
only; I pointed out that even within the concept of
'tactile sensation' we must include those somatic or
haptic sensations that take place inwardly – the
physical stresses of emotion. I paid due attention to
the considerations which led Adolph Hildebrand,
in his famous treatise on the subject, to make a
pictorial presentation of spatial unity the specific
aim of sculpture. But I then asserted – and nothing
has since shaken this conviction – that the art of
sculpture achieves its maximum and most distinctive
effect 'when the sculptor proceeds almost blindly
to the statement of tactile values, values of the
palpable, the ponderable, the assessable mass.'

Integral volume, I declared, not apparent to the eye alone, but given by every direct or imaginable sensation of touch and pressure – such is the unique sculptural emotion.

No wonder that a Constructivist like Gabo, whose works deliberately dispense with mass, are often imponderable and transparent, dependent on a play of light and movement, aerial and intangible – no wonder that such an artist should feel that his work had escaped my definition, and that either my whole historical analysis of the art was false, or that the art he practised must no longer be called sculpture. How is such a contradiction to be resolved?

Let me begin by describing some of the varieties of modern sculpture which do not fit my definition, and let us ask what possible aesthetic justification each of them may possess. Constructivism itself, of which Naum Gabo and his brother Antoine Pevsner are the most typical representatives, had its origins among artists who were not trained as painters or sculptors, but rather as engineers and architects. Gabo himself was trained as an engineer, and has confessed that he came to sculpture imbued with ideas derived from the study of structure and engineering technique. He began to experiment with constructions in the year 1915, in Norway, and when he returned to Moscow in 1917, made contact with a group of artists led by Vladimir Tatlin, an artist who was already practising a form of art based on structural rather than plastic principles. But if we are to trace this new principle of art to its source we must go back to the Italian Futurists, and more particularly to Umberto Boccioni, who already in 1910 had conceived a type of dynamic sculpture, no longer concerned with mass or volume, but with light and movement. Boccioni's ideas were derived from contemporary scientific theories of light, optics and electricity, but Futurism also indulged in an idealization of machinery and speed. Art was conceived as a metaphysical activity, as the transformation of mental concepts into material symbols, and the concepts chosen were no longer religious or idealistic, but rather scientific or technological.

It was not long before these ideas reached Russia – indeed, a Futurist group was founded by the brothers Burljuk in 1910, only a few weeks after the publication of the second Futurist Manifesto in Milan and Turin (the first had been published by Marinetti in 1909). The movement in Moscow thrived and in 1914 was blessed by a personal visit from Marinetti. But like all these early movements in the history of modern art, it soon split into factions, such as the Rayonism of Michael Larionov and the Suprematism of Kasimir Malevich; but these do not concern us now except in so far as they may have affected the basic principles of the art of sculpture.

There is one further decisive innovation to take note of before we have under our observation all the factors that were to contribute to a radical revision of the traditional conception of sculpture. In 1912 Picasso began to experiment by pasting additional textures to the surface of his canvas – paper, oilcloth, even chair-caning – and once he had found the result, which was called a collage, aesthetically satisfying, he proceeded quite logically to make three-dimensional structures on the same principle, using rough pieces of wood, coloured paper, strings and nails. Tatlin, on a visit to Paris in 1913–14, saw these constructions of Picasso's and took the idea back to Moscow, where it combined naturally with the notions already derived from the Futurists.

It is evident that we already have the possibility of two separate developments – one which takes its departure from a mental abstraction such as speed, movement, rhythm, etc., and attempts to represent such an abstraction in a solid structure; and another which takes its departure from the sensuous qualities of ready-made materials in their innocent condition and with these makes an object that represents nothing but is aesthetically satisfying in its appeal. The two developments are somewhat confused at first; Futurism, for example, had renounced beauty and aesthetic appeal: it was an art anti-art. The Constructivists, too, renounced the art of the past; Tatlin called for 'ruthless war against art in general', and all these Russian painters and sculptors thought of their activities as a revolutionary mode of expression consonant with the new world of communism.

The difference, as between Futurism and Constructivism, is that the former was uncompromisingly nihilistic in its intentions, while the latter was in the strict sense of the word revolutionary, wishing to replace the mode of expression called 'art' by a new mode of expression to be called 'tectonics'. The revolution was not confined to materials, as was Picasso's revolution: it was not qualitative, but quantitative; it renounced such quantities as mass and volume; in painting it renounced colour; and in the place of such quantities sought to construct a plastic image that is kinetic rather than massive.

These divergences were already in embryo forty years ago, and have now grown into modes of plastic expression that have nothing in common with each other. Futurism was replaced by Surrealism, and along that line of development, continually inspired by the inventive genius of Picasso, sculpture sought by every means to recover its pristine MAGIC; but in the other direction, rejected by communist politicians, who could only conceive art as pictorial propaganda, Constructivism asserted the absolute and independent values of art, and to these gave the name REALITY. Neither movement, it will be noted, is concerned with the ideal of traditional art, to which we used to give the name BEAUTY.

I propose to trace the consequences of these diverging ideals, but let me first recall the various expressions given to them during the past forty years.

*Pablo Picasso  Glass and Napkin  1914*

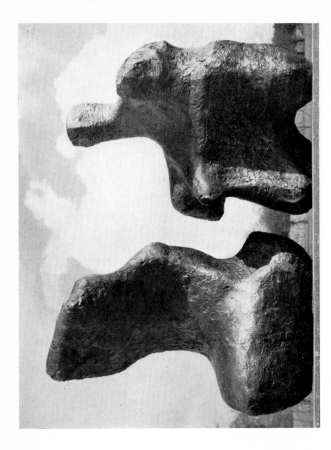

*Henry Moore*
*Two-piece Reclining Figure No. 1  1959*

In the direction of metaphysical realism there could be only one line of development – the search for an ever clearer and ever more precise symbolization of Reality, of what the artist conceives to be an absolute spiritual truth. As a Constructivist like Gabo is never tired of asserting, such an art is in no sense 'abstract': it consists in the concrete or material *images*, and such images are evoked by a sensation of space. Mass, weight and volume are no longer the sculptor's preoccupations, but this all-pervasive mystery of the continuum in which we move and have our being. 'In our sculpture', says Gabo, 'space has ceased to be for us a logical abstraction or a transcendental idea and has become a malleable material element.' Such a preoccupation is not peculiar to the sculptor – it is perhaps the specifically modern preoccupation, shared alike by physicists, architects, engineers and schoolboys. The ambition of our age reaches to the conquest of space, and the Constructivist sculptor has accordingly created the icons of a new *Weltanschauung*. His icons are in no way magical – they are not meant to be expressive of emotions, nor are they in any sense practical. A Constructivist work, Gabo insists, is an image, not a symbol – 'an image of that which was unknown, making it thus known.' In this sense constructive art is a cognitive activity, at the opposite pole to magical art, which is an emotive activity.

In magical art, however, which is the direction

given to sculpture by Picasso, there is an infinite variety of means, but the end is always the same: to convey a secret message or to exercise a mysterious power. Sometimes the message is incised or moulded like runes on a plaque of some kind, or even on a pillar or post as in the case of Henry Moore's *Glenkiln Cross*; in other types the magic is conveyed by means of bent wires and such sculpture differs from Constructivist sculpture only in its evident irrationality. But generally this magical sculpture is figurative, having some more or less direct reference to the human form. The piece of sculpture stands before us like an idol, or like a sooth-sayer uttering prophecies or threats. Eduardo Paolozzi, one of the most powerful creators of these magical (mantic would be a more exact word) images, gives them such names as *The Japanese God of War*, *Her Majesty the Wheel*, *Saint Sebastian*, *Jason*, and *Icarus*, and his intention is clear – the figure is legendary or prophetic, charged with a mysterious destiny. César, Lynn Chadwick, Robert Mueller, Germaine Richier, Giacometti and Moore – all alike seek to recover the animistic vitality of the magical object.

Primitive magic, according to Sir James Frazer, lost its power because it gradually became evident to shrewder intelligences that it did not work: 'Man saw that what he had taken for causes were not causes, and that all his efforts to work by means of these imaginary causes had been vain.' He therefore began to believe in higher and invisible powers that controlled his destiny, 'conscious agents who may be turned from their purpose by persuasion', that is to say, by prayer and propitiation. And so religion was born and prevailed for many centuries. But in our own time we have been taught that the course of nature is determined, 'not by the passions or caprice of personal beings, but by the operation of immutable laws acting mechanically'. Both magic and religion had a use for art, but science, if not indifferent, is antagonistic to its claims to be a symbolic language with access to truth or reality. It is in this situation of dereliction that the artists have returned to the practice of magic. Naturally, the modern magic is far more sophisticated than any of the kinds described in *The Golden Bough*; but in a very real sense the modern sculptor is a public magician, manipulating the characteristic images of a technological civilization.

The images of the modern magician are pre-dominantly mechanistic, but used in such a way that they may dislocate and derange the component 'parts'. Machines that cannot possibly function are found in the iconography of the Dada movement; most prophetic in this sense were the various 'infernal machines' painted or constructed by Marcel Duchamp. From painting mechanized figures, like *The Sad Young Man in a Train* (1911) or the *Nude Descending a Staircase* (1912), Duchamp passed to the painting of actual machines (*The Chocolate Grinder* of 1913) to the construction of absurd machines,

such as the *Cylinder containing a water-mill in neighbouring metals* of 1913–15, and finally to a synthesis
of all this machine-mockery in the large glass
version of *The Bride stripped bare by her Bachelors even*
(1915–23), a work which has been described as 'the
Credo and the last will of Marcel Duchamp'.
What was the credo? His most recent interpreter,
Robert Lebel, describes it in these words: 'His
philosophy was merely that of a pseudo-scientist and
his machines, if we may say so, were only mechan-
isms of the mind. Consequently they expressed
his rejection of the scientific spirit *because it imposes
mechanization in the field of affective relations.*' But it is
not sufficient to repudiate the absolutism of science;
there is then a vacuum to be filled, and Duchamp
was the first to realize that it could be filled only by
a magic that reassembled and reanimated the broken
pieces of the destroyed machine. To impose an
organic life on cogs and wheels, pistons and cylin-
ders – that would be to create a mantic object of
compelling power – in other words, the artist-
magician of the post-scientific age must make use of
mechanistic symbols.

Picasso's use of the debris of our mechanical
civilization is perhaps less obvious, but it is none the
less significant. Prototypes for most of the varieties
of mantic sculpture can be found in his work, notably the iron wire sculpture of 1928, the welded
bronze figure of 1921, and above all, for more recent
developments, the *Goat* of 1950, pieced together

from a wicker-basket, a palm branch, pieces of scrap iron and clay pots, or the *Ape with Young* of 1951, in which various objects such as a toy motor-car are embedded. But Picasso's object is meta-morphosis rather than mockery, and although our first impulse is to be amused by what is in effect a plastic pun, we do not feel the same mockery as in Duchamp. Nevertheless, as Georges Salles has said in writing about the most recent of Picasso's sculptures, the *Baigneurs* of 1957, 'the sculptor's pun is also the magician's language'.

I do not want to give the impression that all the contemporary sculpture that I have described as mantic is obsessed by a mockery of the machine age. The iron sculptures of the Swiss artist, Robert Mueller, though they use up scrap iron and metal waste, are positive creations with little reference to machinery. At the same time, they make use of the typical materials of a mechanized civilization – iron and steel – and submit them to a pre-industrial technique, that of a blacksmith using primitive tools. The same intention is there: to assert the human and erotic will on the insensitive debris of our civilization.

I could cite many other examples of this desire to resurrect a magical phoenix from the scrap-heap of industry, but the few indications I have given are perhaps a sufficient basis for a closer look at this art of a scientific age. The question still arises whether such an art is relevant – whether, that is to say, magic is a commodity that can be conveyed to the disillusioned. This will depend, of course, on our definition of magic, and for a beginning we must rid ourselves of the false notion that magic is a pseudo-science, or in any sense a substitute for science. That notion, typical of Tyler, Frazer and other anthropologists of the last century, has now been replaced by a theory of magic which sees it as much more nearly related to art – as a constructive activity with a specific social function. According to anthropologists like Malinowski and to a philosopher like R. G. Collingwood, magic is not a pseudo-science of any kind, but rather a means to a preconceived end, the end being the arousing of emotion. The means used are artistic; the end is to make the emotions effective agents in the practical life of the community. 'The primary function of all magical arts', says Collingwood, 'is to generate in the agent or agents certain emotions that are considered necessary or useful for the work of living; their secondary function is to generate in others, friends or enemies of the agent, emotions useful or detrimental to the lives of others.' Such functions are not confined to primitive societies; on the contrary, they survive in our so-called civilized societies. 'Magical activity', Collingwood suggests, 'is a kind of dynamo supplying the mechanism of practical life with the emotional current that drives it. Hence magic is a necessity of every sort and condition of man, and is actually found in every healthy society.' He points to many of our daily activities, not only religious ceremonies and military parades, but also fox-hunting and amateur football, as essentially ritual activities undertaken as social duties and surrounded by all the well-known marks and trappings of magic – 'the ritual costume, the ritual vocabulary, the ritual instrument, and above all the sense of electedness, or superiority over the common herd, which always distinguishes the initiate and the hierophant'.

What is significant for our present discussion is that 'magical practices invariably contain, not as peripheral elements but as central elements, artistic activities like dances, songs, drawing or modelling'. Magic produces its effects by representation, and is most effective when the representation is aesthetically vital. Hence the necessity, not merely for a conventional symbol, but for a work of art. I am disagreeing with Collingwood at this point, who suggests that aesthetic standards are irrelevant in magical art, and that the brilliant naturalism of the palaeolithic cave-drawings, for example, cannot be explained by their magical function. On the contrary, their brilliant naturalism must be explained by their urgent necessity in the economy of palaeolithic man: as I have said on another occasion 'a correspondence was established between the efficacy of the image as a symbol . . . and its vividness as a representation of the animal's essence: image corresponded to desire in its intensity, its actuality'.

Even in 1928, when Collingwood published his *Principles of Art,* he could note that 'a recrudescence of magical art is going on before our eyes'. He does not give examples, but he probably had in mind jazz music and dancing as well as the works of painters like Picasso. Thirty years later we can find thousands of examples to illustrate and prove Collingwood's theories. I shall confine myself to magical sculpture, for there can be no doubt that the makers of such sculpture aim to create objects which focus and crystallize emotions that are not so much personal as public, and stand in relation to society, not as representations of the external world, much less as expressions of the artist's personal consciousness or feeling, but rather as catalysts of a collective consciousness. To use a cant phrase, they are conceived as media of mass communication. But obviously what is intended for the masses is not always acceptable to the masses. Even taking this style of sculpture in its most acceptable form, say those figures of Henry Moore which have been interpreted as symbols of the collective archetype known as the Great Mother, there is a vast difference between such isolated symbols and the archetypal symbols proliferated by the film industry and the popular press. The archetypal figure of Marilyn Monroe is worshipped by millions, and her magic is in no sense esoteric; the magic of Henry Moore's sculpture is by comparison the cult of a secret sect.

But so, of course, was the magic of the witch-doctors. Equally esoteric is the magic of those witch-doctors found in the backrooms of Hollywood. The editors of popular magazines and newspapers practise a form of incantation: their victims are passive, unconscious of the enchantments that are being exercised upon them. The modern artist differs from the witch-doctors of the film and the press, not in his intentions, but only in the means employed. He might say that his practice is intensive: that it is not the numbers that matter, but the quality of the audience. In other words, he exercises his magic on an élite, in the belief that this élite, in its turn, will influence and direct the masses. Magic has its hierarchy, and the masses are swayed by the initiated few.

A dangerous doctrine, with unpleasant political implications. Magic, we are reminded, is potent for evil as well as for good, and what assurance have we that the magic practised by modern sculptors is beneficial? To release demons from the personal unconscious may be an act of therapy, as blood-letting used to be. But why exhibit our personal demons to the public? It is precisely at this point that art becomes subject to social control, for if the purpose of magical art is, as Collingwood says, to canalize emotion and direct it upon practical life, then its ends must be defined by social needs. I have already hinted at what those ends might be: to restore that sense of the numinous that has been destroyed by the rational tradition. If, as one critic has maintained, we are literally at the end of thought, having reached that abomination of desolation which William Blake saw prophetically as the final outcome of an abstract objecting power that negatives everything, the same condition that Kierkegaard described as 'the Sickness unto Death'; if we have really reached this stage of intellectual futility, then a magical art may be considered as a cunning attempt to make art socially effective, and thereby find some issue from the rationalistic impasse. A dangerous enterprise, but who will deny its necessity? In a community that is rotten with amusement, Collingwood suggested, the more magic we produce the better. 'If we were talking about the moral regeneration of our world, I should urge the deliberate creation of a system of magic, using as its vehicles such things as the theatre and the profession of letters, as one indispensable kind of means to that end.' But Collingwood went on to point out that magic in itself is not art, for art has a function of its own that is not magical. Magic makes use of art, as does religion or political propaganda or commercial advertising, and that is why a magical art, for all its power to enchant us, must remain ambiguous. Any art is ambiguous, Collingwood maintains, that issues from a consciousness clouded by an unartistic purpose, magical, religious, political or social. Art itself, unambiguous art, proceeds from a consciousness that has no other content but the emotion that is to be expressed.

But what then of the other kind of modern sculpture, tectonic sculpture? Must that too be excluded from the true tradition? Is it also an ambiguous art? The question is more difficult to answer in this case, simply because the tectonic sculptor, who is no less aware of the rationalistic impasse, seeks an egress in intuition, and intuition is an elusive faculty, part intellect and part emotion. In magical art emotion is expressed by means of symbols which even when most abstract are archetypal – that is to say, they are drawn from remote racial experiences, from the collective unconscious. But in tectonic art there are no symbols in this sense: but only created images – not archetypes from the past, but prototypes of the future. The structural ideal represented by tectonic art is an objective image of the truth: of the structural truth inherent in materials, of the structural truth as represented by such elements as harmony, symmetry, 'organic' proportions and rhythmical movement. There are no demons in this world: only shapes, lines, colours, forms that have factual existence and kinetic energy. Their impact on our senses, is, in the words of Naum Gabo, 'as real as the impact of light or of an electric shock. This impact can be verified in the way that we verify any other natural phenomenon. Shapes, colours and lines speak their own language. They are events in themselves and in an organized construction they become beings – the psychological force is immediate, irresistible and universal to all species of mankind; not being the result of a convention as words are, they are unambiguous and it is for this reason that their impact can influence the human psyche; it can break or mould it, it exults, it depresses, elates or makes desperate; it can bring order where there was confusion and it can disturb and exasperate where there was an order.' The overriding purpose of this kind of art is to create and convey a well-organized and clearly defined image, 'which by its very existence as a plastic vision should provoke in us the forces and the desires to enhance life, assert it and assist its further development'.

A magical art and a tectonic art thus stand opposed as agencies of the creative spirit, one attempting to arouse and concentrate human emotions in ritual obedience to some idea of social unity; the other presenting images that discipline these same emotions for some constructive purpose. The distinction is basically that which divides all manifestations of the human spirit into dialectical opposition, the eternal conflict of inner and outer, of subjective and objective states of mind, of romanticism and classicism, of vitality and beauty – the dialectic is endless. But if what seems so strange and revolutionary in the art of our time resolves into the eternal antithesis of the human condition, in what sense can the sculpture we have been considering be said to differ from the sculpture of the past? In what sense are the symbols of magic and the images of tectonics different from the symbols and images of ancient art? Only, I would suggest, in their superficial manifestations. Obviously the magical figures of a Giacometti or a Paolozzi do not differ essentially from the magical figures we find in ancient Etruscan sculpture or in the tribal sculpture of the Congo; and the plastic images of a Gabo or a Pevsner do not differ essentially from the organized shapes, lines and columns we find in a Greek temple or a Sung vase. Our modern belief is that the manifestations of the creative spirit cannot be reduced to a unity: we should be grateful for their prolific variety. Nevertheless, if there are a few in our midst who seek for such an ideal unity, for a perfect law in art, it will be found in only one or two rare masterpieces, that find a synthesis beyond the magical and the tectonic. Ruskin thought he had found such perfect law in what he called a piece of 'mathematic sculpture', the tomb of Ilaria del Caretto in Lucca Cathedral, carved in the year 1406 by Jacopo della Quercia; of which he wrote* that it is the only piece of monumental work known to him in the world 'which unites in perfect and errorless balance the softest mysteries of emotion with the implacable severities of science'. It may be felt that there are no soft mysteries in the magical sculpture of to-day, and that the severities of our

* 'The Schools of Art in Florence' Lecture V. *The Works of John Ruskin*, Vol. XXIII, pp. 221-36.

tectonic sculpture are too implacable. No single work stands out in our time with such commanding 'reserve and restraint of power' as this work of the Renaissance. Unambiguous unity of this perfection is, indeed, a rare achievement in any period.

The mysteries of emotion may be there – they are surely present in the magical sculpture of our time; the severities of science may be there, and they are surely present in the tectonic sculpture of our time. But these two kinds of modern sculpture are divided in their aims, in their techniques, and in their effects; and so long as they are thus divided, the ideal of unity must be renounced.

# THE SOCIAL SIGNIFICANCE OF
## ABSTRACT ART

IT IS NOW half a century since the abstract movement in art made its first tentative appearance. It was for many years attacked by critics, ridiculed by the man in the street, ignored by collectors and museums, but in spite of all discouragement, amounting sometimes to persecution and often involving financial sacrifice, the number of artists practising some sort of abstraction has continued to increase and their work now enjoys a certain measure of popularity. As a movement, abstract art is a world-wide phenomenon and is not likely to disappear. Indeed, it may be said that it has become the academicism of our time, and most young artists regard it as the normal mode of expression in painting and sculpture. What is the explanation of this extraordinary revolution in art that has taken place in our time?

Let us first decide what we mean by the word 'abstract'. If we consult a dictionary we discover that it means 'separated from matter, practice, or particular examples, not concrete'; and that indeed was the original application of the word to works of art. It was used to describe paintings which had drawn from the particular object in front of the artist an *essence* which in his opinion was nearer to the truth than any mechanical representation of its appearance. The intention to find an essential reality beyond the retinal image began with Cézanne, who felt that there was something false and impermanent about a direct visual impression such as the Impressionists had vainly tried to render. He wished to 'realize' (that is to say, reveal and clarify) the basic structure of things. Cézanne was concerned with his sensuous apprehension of the object in front of him, in all its concreteness. An ambiguity that has confused all discussion of the subject begins at this point, for Cézanne thought that the essential quality of an object was its concreteness; nothing, therefore, *abstracted* from nature. Cézanne's desire was to be more realistic than his predecessors; 'essence' he would have regarded as a question for philosophers, not artists.

The next stage in the evolution towards abstract art is represented by Cubism. This movement was based partly on the structural simplicity of Cézanne's paintings, partly on the geometrical simplification found in African tribal sculpture, which was discovered around 1908 by Picasso and his friends. Picasso described African sculpture as *raisonnable*, which in French means having to do with conception rather than perception, in other words, with thought rather than vision. The artist begins with an idea and tries to give it visual form – the idea of a god, or of a ghost, or of the spirit of an animal. Cubism was not inspired by the same animistic

*Henry Moore*
*Four-piece Reclining Figure 1934*

*Henry Moore  Glenkiln Cross  1955-56*

motives, but it took the artistic effects (notably a flattening out of the surface planes in sculpture), combined these with an analytical sense of underlying structures derived from Cézanne, and the result was the style we call 'cubist'. But it was not yet abstraction. There was always a concrete object at the back of the artist's mind; and when Picasso and Braque saw in what direction their experiments were leading, they drew back in alarm. 'There is no abstract art', Picasso declared. 'You must always start with something. Afterwards you can remove all traces of reality. There's no danger then, anyway, *because the idea of the object will have left an indelible mark.*'

But all artists did not agree with Picasso. Juan Gris, who began to experiment alongside Picasso and Braque from 1911, soon saw other possibilities in Cubism. Briefly, he gradually abandoned the analytical and descriptive approach, to substitute a method that might be called synthetic and formal. There was no theoretical basis to his method, but he tended to use 'a series of unrelated, arbitrary, angular and modular relationships and proportions to carry out his cubist displacements and his cubist analysis of volumes with a feeling of greater explicitness and exactitude'.* Gris never abandoned the object, but he distorted it almost beyond recognition, and completed the picture-space by the use of geometrical areas of colour determined by the

* John Golding: *Cubism*, London 1959, p. 131.

formal unity of the composition as a whole. He claimed to be able to reduce any given composition to purely geometric terms. Other artists – Gleizes, Delaunay, Mondrian – came along and said, in effect, why bother with an object: if the proportions are good and the colours harmonious, they suffice for a work of art: the *representation* of a concrete object, a *motif*, was irrelevant. The picture was, so to speak, its own *motif*, a thing of beauty and a joy for ever.

Thus abstract art was born – but only one kind of abstract art. At the same time that these developments were taking place in Paris, parallel developments were taking place in Munich. There art had followed the course of events in Paris – impressionism, post-impressionism, and even, under the direct influence of Paris, the first phases of cubism. But there was a separate current in Germany, coming from the North, the expressionism of Munch, Van Gogh, Rohlfs and Nolde, based on feeling rather than thought, using colour to express emotion in the most direct and brutal manner. But expressionism, too, was influenced by primitive African and Oceanic art, and to this extent shared one of the sources of cubism.

The incident belongs to the mythology of the modern movement and must be retold. One day in 1908, Kandinsky, a Russian painter working in Munich, came back to his studio and saw on the easel an unfamiliar painting – glowing with colour, expressive in form, but representing nothing. It was one of his own expressionistic paintings which he had left on its side, and which he therefore did not immediately recognize. This experience was to Kandinsky an apocalyptic flash of illumination: the painting as it stood there in its incomprehensibility was more moving than it had been in its proper position. He began to experiment, using touches of colour and non-representational forms, to create 'symbols of inner necessity'. He combined these forms into paintings which he called 'improvisations', a word often used for musical compositions. Kandinsky was a friend of the composer Schönberg, and had often discussed with him the aims of their separate arts, as expressed in sound and in vision, and he had come to the conclusion that these aims were fundamentally the same, to express an inner emotional state – to find satisfaction for vague feelings in precise forms. But it was not until he saw his painting on its side that he suddenly felt that this aim could be more perfectly realized if the painter was not concerned with the different and possibly irrelevant aim of representing a concrete object – a landscape or a portrait. The real landscape was in the soul.

We thus have two separate origins for two distinct types of abstract art. Critics have never been able to agree on the appropriate names for these types, but one is essentially *expressionist*, based on emotion, and the other is essentially *constructivist*, based on formal intuition. The constructivist may argue that in the result his work of art involves the emotions and expresses an inner state of feeling; the expressionist may argue that in the result his work of art achieves formal relations and colour-harmonies without which there would be no aesthetic appeal. The public may conclude that the name does not matter so long as the result is a work of art.

In the course of the last fifty years there has been an intense development of these two types of abstraction, but though they sometimes constitute separate schools, such as *De Stijl* in Holland, or Action Painting in the United States, there is no decisive departure from the original types of abstraction. It is sometimes suggested that the movement known in the United States as Action Painting is a new development because the artist is concerned not to express an inner state of feeling, but rather to extend the field of his physical awareness. His activity has no basis in emotion, but is rather an exercise as impersonal and as enjoyable as fencing or skating. But this, I believe, is a distinction without a difference: though the action painter may have no intention of expressing emotion, nevertheless he generates it, and the result, from the spectator's point of view, may be equally effective. Every gesture we make, whether we are skating or painting with a brush, signing a letter or dribbling colours on to a canvas from a pierced can (said to be the method sometimes used by Jackson Pollock) is 'expressive'. Expressive of what? Perhaps not of an 'inner necessity' such as Kandinsky felt, perhaps of nothing that could be described as spiritual or metaphysical; expressive just of the artist's personality, but of that personality seeking some security in the outer world, some communion with other people – a life-line, as it were, thrown out into a sea where there is no anchorage.

This brings us to the heart of the subject. We can trace the evolution of art towards abstraction step by step, and as a development it seems logical enough. A retrospective exhibition of one of the pioneers of abstract art (such as Piet Mondrian) will show how slowly and tentatively each step was taken. Between one painting and another, between the work of one year and the work of the next, there is a scarcely discernible difference. But slowly the natural object, a tree or a church, is modified. Lines are interrupted, shapes dissolve, colours are broken down and their constituent elements separated and purified; until over a period of five or six years we lose all sense of the original object, and what was at first entitled *The Church at Domburg*, becomes first *Church Façade* (it is no longer possible to identify any particular church) and then perhaps *Façade* (for even a church is no longer evident), and finally *Composition*, for there is no longer any trace of the object left.

But Picasso would say there is still the *idea* of the object, and that the composition could not have existed unless the church tower at Domburg had made an indelible impression on Mondrian's vision, on his mind. That is perhaps true of Mondrian's paintings up to about 1916, but then he began to experiment with lines and colour planes, not 'starting with something in reality', unless lines and colours are said to be 'reality'. In all the discussion of abstract art one continually falls into such semantic traps. By 'reality' Picasso meant a 'given' reality, trees and churches and other such environmental objects; but when, after 1916, Mondrian spoke of 'reality' he meant a 'created' reality, a reality that comes into existence, or is discovered for the first time by the artist when he establishes certain relations between lines and colours. In 1912–20 he wrote a long essay in dialogue form to make clear this distinction between 'natural reality' and 'abstract reality'.

The usual supposition is that abstract art is a flight from reality, but this Mondrian and all the pioneers of abstract art have fiercely denied. Historically it can be argued (this is the thesis of Wilhelm Worringer, whose essay on *Abstraction and Empathy* was published in Munich in 1908, the year of Kandinsky's apocalyptic experience) that the tendency to make art unnatural, geometric, abstract, is a tendency found in periods when, or in climates where, the environment is against man. He retreats from the brutal facts of life into a world of abstract harmony which does not remind him of these facts. Far from wishing to 'represent' life, his only desire is to forget it, and to find peace and security in a realm of transcendental bliss.

Since our modern world fits the historical explanation only too well, it is logical to apply this hypothesis to modern abstract art. We live in an age of anxiety, of war and revolution; what could be more natural than to retreat into a world of beauty, expressed in rhythmical lines and harmonious colours, far from the madding crowd of visual impressions that assault our sensibilities if we look around us?

I believe that this is a correct but superficial explanation for the appearance of abstract art in our time; it is not an adequate explanation of its development and its present universal appeal. If abstract art were merely a flight from reality, it would be a negative thing, of little value to mankind. But all the evidence suggests that abstract art is a positive thing, dynamic and creative. Compared with the academic art of the nineteenth century, it is intensely dynamic, and inspires an almost religious devotion in its practitioners and disciples. What is the source of its positive appeal?

It is easy to invent metaphysical explanations – to say that abstract art is an expression of man's desire to be in 'tune with the universe'. Mondrian often used that kind of explanation – for example:

'Plastic vision implies action; by plastic vision, we destroy the natural experience, and reconstruct that appearance abstractly. Our plastic vision so to speak corrects our habitual, natural vision – thus we reduce the individual to the universal with which we become united.' But Mondrian also used very practical explanations. He was fond of dancing, and the two last great paintings of his life, painted in New York, *Broadway Boogie-Woogie* and *Victory Boogie-Woogie*, are evidence of this passion. He found a parallel to abstract art in modern dancing, more particularly in modern dance steps.

In the old style of dancing, the music and the steps of the dance flowed into each other; the movement of the dance might be represented by a curved line. In modern dancing, one dances *against* the music. Two elements are balanced: there is an opposition between the rhythm and the melody of the music, and a corresponding opposition in the steps of the dance – no longer a curve, but a straight line. This may be a fanciful comparison, but Mondrian meant to illustrate the fact that vitality itself comes from the balance of opposed forces: that art, like life, is the expression of a complementarity. The modern movement has discovered the essential dialectical character of art: the unity that is achieved by resolving contradictions. Rhythm and stability, direction and position, colour and shape, horizontal and vertical – all these elements are opposed to each other within the unity of the work of art.

Such unity, a unity that is *in* art as it is *in* reality, is not an escape from chaos and anxiety, but is achieved by a refinement of vision, by what is in effect an extension of visual sensibility; and Mondrian believed that such a new vision was the basis for a new society. It is significant that the greatest admirers of Mondrian, as of the Constructivist sculptors Gabo and Pevsner, are architects, for they perceive the connection between what we might call the constructive vision of the artist and the practical vision of the architect, which might also be called constructive. Indeed, there is no distinction, except that of scale, between the work of a Mondrian and the work of an architect like Mies van der Rohe: both belong to what Mondrian has called 'a society based on the equation of the material and the spiritual, a society composed of balanced relationships'. Mies has used almost identical words: 'In its simplest form architecture is rooted in entirely functional considerations, but it can reach up through all degrees of value to the brightest sphere of spiritual existence, into the realm of pure art'.

By concentrating on Mondrian and what is sometimes called 'pure' abstraction I may seem to have left the other kind of abstract art, abstract expressionism, without an explanation, but I do not think so. All these new tendencies in art have been ascribed, as Mondrian noted, to greater consciousness of the fourth dimension. I am not sure that many artists would be able to give an adequate account of the fourth dimension, but we are all conscious of the problems of time and space as revealed (but not solved) by modern physics, and artists have something to say about such problems. In one direction (the direction of Mondrian and Gabo) the solutions (they are not identical) are found *against* the music – the synthesis is found in a determined balance, in unified relationships. In the other direction (the direction of Pollock and De Kooning) the synthesis is found *without* the music: that is to say, by an indeterminate leap into space itself, as if to discover there the nature of infinity. Action Painting might therefore be defined as a plastic speculation on the nature of infinity.

There is one further refinement to note before we have surveyed all the varieties of abstraction. Perhaps as an extension of Action Painting, perhaps as a return to Picasso's belief that the artist 'must always start with something', and more precisely as a result of a new appreciation of Monet's 'immense and mysterious' renderings of water landscapes, a somewhat revised version of abstract impressionism has appeared, especially in the United States. The aim is not so much to remove gradually all traces of reality, in the manner of some of the early Cubists, but rather to give a direct rendering of the artist's immediate sensations in the presence of natural objects. Such immediate sensations are not realistic; Monet complained that the sun set too fast for him to render the 'instantaneity' of the effects he sought to render; and Kandinsky, after seeing one of Monet's Haystacks in 1895, described very accurately the effects that the abstract impressionists of to-day are still trying to achieve:

'Suddenly, for the first time, I saw a "picture". That it was a haystack, the catalogue informed me. I could not recognize it. This lack of recognition was distressing to me. I also felt that the painter had no right to paint so indistinctly. I had a muffled sense that the object was lacking in this picture, and was overcome with astonishment and perplexity that it not only seized, but engraved itself indelibly on the memory and, quite unexpectedly, again and again, hovered before the eyes down to the smallest detail. All of this was unclear to me, and I could not draw the simple consequences from this experience. But what was absolutely clear to me was the unsuspected power, previously hidden from me, of the palette, which surpassed all my dreams. Painting took on a fabulous strength and splendour. And at the same time, unconsciously, the object was discredited as an indispensable element of the picture. . . .'

'The object was discredited' – that is the essential point, and the object remains discredited in recent developments of abstract impressionism. The names of Mark Tobey and (in his recent work) Milton Reznik will perhaps indicate more precisely the type of abstraction to which I am referring.

247

We may conclude from this brief survey of the varieties of abstract art that have developed throughout the world during the past fifty years that however much they may differ in style and technique, the motivation is the same: to discredit the object as a given aspect of the reality to be represented by the artist and to substitute in its place an abstract image which the artist presents as 'discovered' or 'essential' reality. But we are still seeking for an adequate explanation of a development that has no precedent in the history of art.

Previous explanations of a will to abstraction, such as those of Lipps, Riegl and Worringer, are in my opinion too limited to account for what is a universal phenomenon. Such explanations rely either on local geographical factors (such as the 'oasis' culture of Egypt) or on climatic factors (the cold and inclement North). Although Worringer uses the terms *abstraction* and its antithesis *empathy* in a generic sense, in his historical perspective he is compelled to restrict himself to local manifestations such as 'the Northern artistic volition' or 'Oriental transcendental inclinations'. Worringer, in his epoch-making thesis, deliberately sets out to disprove the assumption that any general formula, such as 'aesthetic enjoyment is objectified self-enjoyment', can explain all the artistic creations of many ages and peoples, and in this he succeeds. Worringer took over from a brilliant Viennese scholar, Alois Riegl, the idea of an '*a priori* existent absolute artistic volition', or, more briefly, a will to form, which is modified by the circumstances of time and place. The extremes of such modification are organic naturalism, characteristic of the Greek civilization, and geometrical abstraction, characteristic of primitive peoples and of certain culturally developed Oriental peoples. The task of the historian of art is to explain the stylistic variations of a basic will-to-art in terms of the material conditions in which it is manifested and by which it is modified. He can succeed admirably in his task (as does Worringer) so long as a variation of styles corresponds to a variation of material conditions. But the situation we are now confronted with is the creation of a stylistic unity, namely abstraction, that overrides many variations of social environment.

Before attempting to explain this new phenomenon, let me briefly dispose of one possible objection. It might be suggested that there is no absolute universality of abstract art in our time since two great countries, Russia and China, still resist its charms. To this one must reply that an *a priori* artistic volition is only absolute so long as it is allowed to develop in political freedom. Any river can be dammed – for a time. The cultural dams have broken in Yugoslavia and Poland; they are already leaking in Hungary and Czechoslovakia; even in Russia and China they cannot forever withstand spiritual pressures that dominate the whole world. Perhaps this will be more evident when the *a priori* nature of these spiritual pressures has been defined.

Let us first ask whether there are any world-wide material conditions that might account for a universal will to abstraction. The first that might occur to us is the almost universal mechanization of the processes of production, and this phenomenon does indeed merit our careful consideration. Mechanization, and the division of labour that goes with it, is an affront to our humanity, which is normally nurtured and reproduced by organic processes. How often, through our greatest spiritual leaders, we have protested against mechanization and the alienation of man. Ruskin and Marx, Nietzsche and Bergson, Tolstoy and Lawrence, Jaspers and Schweitzer, Gandhi and Vinoba, they speak with one voice, prophetic of doom. It would be inconceivable that such a fundamental revolution in the life of mankind should not have had a profound effect on man's artistic volition. Is this the single and adequate explanation of the phenomenon that confronts us in all its magnitude and mystery?

It is surely a great part of the explanation, especially if we trace the reaction, not on the superficial level of mechanized living (potent as this might be as a superficial influence on the forms of art), but on the deeper levels known since Marx first used the word as *alienation (Entfremdung)*. Alienation is, indeed, the word also used by Worringer to describe Northern man's reaction to an unfriendly or inclement environment of a natural kind; how much more appropriate, therefore, as a word to describe universal man's reaction to an environment that is not merely organically inclement, but positively unnatural? But alienation itself is not a superficial or merely sensational reaction: it is a process involving the mind and spirit of man in their most intimate recesses. It is a social psychosis, a metaphysical disease. Its social effects have often been described by sociologists, by pioneers like Adam Smith and Karl Marx, by contemporary sociologists like Hannah Arendt and David Riesman; its spiritual effects never more eloquently than by Ruskin, significantly when discussing the 'savageness' of Gothic art. 'Men', he wrote, 'were not intended to work with the accuracy of tools, to be precise and perfect in all their actions. If you will have that precision out of them, and make their fingers measure degrees like cog-wheels, and their arms strike curves like compasses, you must un-humanize them. All the energy of their spirits must be given to make cogs and compasses of themselves. All their attention and strength must go to the accomplishment of the mean act. The eye of the soul must be bent upon the finger-point, and the soul's force must fill all the invisible nerves that guide it, ten hours a day, that it may not err from its steely precision, and so soul and sight be worn away, and the whole human being be lost at last – a heap of sawdust, so far as its intellectual work in this world is concerned: saved only by its Heart, which cannot go into the form of cogs and compasses, but expands, after the ten hours are over, into fireside humanity.' When work is 'a perpetual and exquisitely timed palsy', then art, which is the only freedom left to mankind, must expand into savage liberty.

There are two possible objections to such a theory of action and reaction. Is it not true, in the first place, that modern art has to a considerable extent been inspired by the 'engineering rationality' of our time? If the idealization of the machine by the Futurists is in the objector's mind, then I would say that their work ought to be interpreted as a protest against academic realism rather than as 'machine art'; at any rate, it was soon to turn, in the significant work of Marcel Duchamp, into machine mockery. Nevertheless, the movement had its serious, even its metaphysical elements, and these were to inspire Tatlin and other precursors of the Constructivist movement in Russia. It is true that, as it developed, this latter movement, in the work of Gabo and Pevsner, left the machine and all utilitarian tectonics far behind it, to concentrate on the invention of new images of reality – an intuitive spiritual enterprise far removed from engineering rationality. But it can be said with truth that engineering and machinery generally had made the artist more fully aware of certain kinetic elements – movement and rhythm, for example – and modern art, which can be characterized in a certain general sense as dynamic (as opposed to the static character of Greek art), may have been influenced in this sense by its mechanistic environment. But the opposite thesis would be tenable: namely, that the sense of movement that characterized the art of the Baroque period – the steam engine, we should remember, was an invention of this period – inspired, however sub-consciously, the first machines.

The other possible objection is that the reaction in art is far too partial to correspond to a phenomenon so widespread as mechanization: the machine is so universal and so penetrates every recess of life, that the reaction should be universal too, and not confined to an artistic coterie. But the reaction is by no means confined to the arts or to a coterie of artists: it shows up equally in the desperate search for leisure and amusement, in the unprecedented development of tourism, motoring, camping, sport, any escape from the perpetual and exquisitely timed palsy of our technological civilization. It is not realistic to expect a general appreciation of reactions that are first manifested in the fine arts. One can find grosser aesthetic reactions in so-called 'pop-art' which in an industrial civilization is a substitute for folk art: strip cartoons, westerns, the Hollywood film; these are in no sense a positive reaction to a congenial environment; on the contrary, they represent an impulse to self-alienation as powerful and as apprehensive as the urge to abstraction. The need for empathy, for objectified self-enjoyment, is satisfied in idealized archetypes (the dumb blonde, the epicene crooner, the heroic gangster) as remote from daily life on the assembly line as is a painting by Mondrian from a tree in the park.

To characterize abstract art as a reaction to the mechanization of the means of production is not to remove art from the realm of reality. On the contrary, art constitutes for man the only certain reality, for reality is what we discover by our senses and shape by our intelligence. Its frontiers are continually under revision, and each step into unknown territory is established by some new intuition, some fresh image, some dimension first realised in the plastic forms of art. Art is a dialectical process, a process, in the words of Marx, 'in which man of his own accord starts, regulates, and controls the material reactions between himself and nature'. Art is a sensuous human activity that gives man a reasoned relation to the surrounding world, and I see nothing in the origins, scope and development of abstract art in our time that does not correspond to this dialectical conception of the process. Mechanization has taken command of our economic activities, but for that very reason the artistic will of man manifests the greatest freedom it has ever known.

# WHY ABSTRACT?

IT IS EXACTLY half a century since the first abstract pictures were painted (by Kandinsky). During that time the abstract movement has continued to grow, until now it is the non-abstract or representational painters who are in a minority – at least, among the painters of the younger generation. And yet the abstract artists (we must remember that sculptors as well as painters are involved) have not carried a majority of the public with them. Perhaps the gap between the *avant-garde* and the main body of educated taste is always wide, but we may doubt if it has ever been as wide as it is to-day. In spite of the high esteem which abstract art enjoys among collectors, and the fantastic prices paid for it in the salerooms, the man in the street remains bewildered, sometimes angry, often indifferent. He has an obstinate feeling that his leg is being pulled, that the abstract artist cannot really expect to be taken seriously, that the whole business is a racket of some kind.

What are the main charges brought against the abstract movement? They were formulated for me by the editor of a New York magazine, and I answered them one by one, in the following words:

1. *It fails to communicate any meaning, representing only the artist talking to himself.*

C. K. Ogden and I. A. Richards wrote a famous book called *The Meaning of Meaning*, but this dealt with problems of language and logic. A similar problem exists in the plastic arts. What is the 'meaning' of a painting or a piece of sculpture? Only the most simple people would suggest that the meaning of the picture is the story it tells – that a work of art should be the description of a scene or the narration of an event. Tolstoy, who was not a simple person, asserted that the value of the work of art lies in its truth; and Ruskin, though he had a different conception of the truth, argued in much the same way. The socialist realists of Russia adopt this same argument. Art for them, as for Tolstoy and Ruskin, is a means of communicating a message of some kind, about social conditions, about natural phenomena, about human relations, and it is implied that what should be communicated by the work of art is understanding.

At this point we encounter a philosophical problem. Is understanding a rational process, the kind of discourse or mode of communication that should be confined to logical statements in words; or is it possibly an irrational process, the kind of statement that can only be made by the use of visual symbols?

The defender of abstract art believes that art in

general is a form of symbolic discourse, and that even when it is representational, its message is conveyed by form and colour rather than by the imitation of the things we see. He points out that other arts, such as music and architecture, do not imitate anything in nature, but communicate by abstract arrangements of sounds, intervals, proportions and rhythms. There is no reason why the arrangements of lines and colours on a canvas, or of mass and volume in a piece of sculpture, should not be abstract in the same way. It is merely a convention, of limited historical significance, to maintain that the visual arts should communicate their meaning by imitating the arbitrary forms that nature has evolved. Music might just as logically be confined to the imitation of bird-songs or thunder; architecture to the imitation of caves and mountains.

The abstract work of art may be a riddle, but it is not meaningless: it is a symbol which may stand for the artist's deepest emotions and intuitions, and in which the spectator may find his own emotions and intuitions defined and illuminated.

2. *There are no standards of judgement in abstract art, either of imagery or technique. Anyone – even a child – can paint an abstract painting. Mere doodling may be offered as abstract art. Thus, it becomes impossible to tell a good abstract painting from a bad one.*

What is a standard of judgement in art? Presumably the visual images given in our perception of the external world. Again a philosophical problem is involved, for there is no standard image of the external world. The way in which we see things is a product of learning and interpretation. The image of the external world which we have at any moment is a convention, and varies from age to age, and even from individual to individual. This is evident enough from the history of art – each period has its own method of constructing an image of the external world; there is little in common between an image of the Byzantine period and an image of the Classical Renaissance. The image of man varies not only from age to age but also from artist to artist. What is a standard image of man? The ancient Chinese had one image, the Greeks another. Some religions create an image of the ideal man; others, such as the Mohammedan, forbid the representation of such an ideal (for only God is perfect, and it would be presumptuous of man to consider himself capable of representing such perfection).

One kind of abstract artist, like the Islamic artist, believes that there is an ideal of perfection, but it is impersonal: that is to say, a question of quantitative harmony – the rhythmical succession of lines, the balance of areas, the harmonious unity of colours, the organic articulation of space. Another kind of abstract artist seeks an image that may or may not have such concrete quantities, but is essentially expressive of emotion, or has some inexplicable magical quality. There are shapes that appeal to us for no rational reason – the graining of wood, the eroded pebbles on a beach, cloud formations, sunsets, blots of ink, flotsam from the sea. The Chinese and Japanese take great irregular pieces of rock and erect them in their gardens because they have a strange animistic power or charm. Form is as mysterious as life itself. The artist is a man who reveals the mystery of form.

Even the child as it scribbles can do this. An American teacher, Rhoda Kellogg of the Golden Gate Nursery School, San Francisco, has classified children's scribbles and revealed their symbolic significance. A comparison of abstract art with children's scribbles does not make abstract art ridiculous; on the contrary, it connects it organically with the beginnings of all visual symbols.

As for technique, much as this may baffle the critic of abstract art, I would say that the standard is the same as in representational art. It is a question of the artist's skill in using his tools and his materials to their best advantage. There are badly painted abstract pictures just as there are badly painted representational pictures; and there are well painted pictures of each kind. Even spontaneity, which is characteristic of the brush-strokes in abstract expressionist painting, is also found in representational painting – in Tiepolo or Magnasco, in the Impressionists and the Expressionists.

In abstract art and in representational art, the standards are the same. There is only good art and bad art. Coherent composition, sensibility to colour harmonies, rhythmic movement and significant imagery – abstract art possesses all the essentially aesthetic qualities that have been present in the art of the past. An English painter who is not abstract has made this point in words he would allow me to quote: 'Those of us whose work no one, I imagine, would call "abstract", know, nevertheless, that it is an abstract *quality*, however hidden or devious, which determines the real worth of any work.'*

*3. It represents novelty for novelty's sake. There is a primary concern with being 'different' that leads to mere sensationalism. There is a difference between a movement and a cult. Abstract art is a fashionable cult.*

It is true that modern art of all kinds, including poetry and music, has been deliberately concerned to 'make it new'. At the most general and perhaps profoundest level, this is a reflection of our historical situation. We live in a revolutionary period, and the changes in art are but a reflection of the changes in society. But the position is more paradoxical than this generalization implies, for to-day the most revolutionary societies – those of Russia and China – are the most conservative in their arts. This, I believe, can be fully explained by the rise of a revolutionary dictatorship with little understanding of the conditions in which art flourishes, with

* David Jones: *Epoch and Artist* (Faber), London, 1959

the result that many of the best artists in these countries (Stravinsky, Kandinsky, Chagall) escaped to become leaders of the modern movement in other countries.

More direct explanations of the novel elements in modern art are to be found in the scientific and technical discoveries of our time. The invention of photography and the moving picture had a profound effect on the art of painting. So did technical advances in speed, the new dimensions of space given by the airplane, the new world of form revealed by the microscope. Form itself was established as a guiding principle in nature, in the universe, and form inevitably (and perhaps unconsciously) became the preoccupation of the artist. It would be absurd to complain of novelty for novelty's sake in science: it is equally absurd to complain of it in art. Art has merely kept in step with a changing world, and the more art has changed the more it has remained the same thing: the symbolic representation of reality.

The suggestion that such an activity constitutes a 'cult' is far from the truth. There have been cults in the past – the Pre-Raphaelite Brotherhood was one, and in our own time the Surrealist movement had some of the characteristics of a cult (rigid rules, manifestoes of aims, organs of propaganda, etc.). Abstract art, by contrast, is one of the most universal movements in the history of art. It is practised in every country in the world apart from Russia and China (even communist countries like Poland,

Czechoslavakia and Yugoslavia have active movements). And there are no rules. Abstract art can accommodate all varieties of human temperament and expression, from the severe classicism of a Mondrian to the wild romanticism of a de Kooning.

*4. It is mere decoration, no more profound than a pattern for wall paper or draperies. Does not the abstract artist work first towards the effect of his canvas on a museum wall (witness the enormous size of abstract expressionist canvasses) rather than towards the intensification of experience?*

Ruskin once said that all great art is essentially decorative. The great compositions of Titian, Michelangelo, Rubens, are 'decorative'. In the same manner the paintings of Kandinsky, Mondrian, Nicholson or Pollock are decorative. If the abstract artist 'works first towards the effect of his canvas on the wall', he is doing exactly what Titian, Michelangelo and Rubens did. What is exceptional in the history of painting is the small 'cabinet' picture so popular with bourgeois collectors. The modern painter wishes to be emancipated from this convention of the past century or two, and to return to the 'grand manner' of the great painters of the past. He may not be wise to limit his market in this way, but he is demanding the full scale of his medium. We do not expect architects to restrict themselves to the building of cottages, or musicians to the composition of songs.

It is true that some abstract compositions are

empty, but that is because they are poor compositions, not because they are abstract. 'Intensification
of experience' is not a question of size, but of the
effectiveness of the symbols used. Any Gothic
cathedral will serve as an illustration of intense
grandeur; and, in its overall effect, of abstract
spatial expression.

5. *It is devoid of human emotion. It has no philosophical
foundation, no concern with basic and permanent values, as
great art has always had.*

No art could have deeper philosophical foundations.
Works like Worringer's *Abstraction and Empathy*,
Kandinsky's *Art of Spiritual Harmony*, Mondrian's
*Plastic Art*, the writings of Gabo, Malevich, Klee,
all these constitute a wealth of speculation on the
principles of art without rival in history. All these
writings are concerned with 'basic and permanent
values', and such values are human values.

Nevertheless, the charge that abstract art is
'devoid of human emotion' has some force if by
human emotion is meant the day-to-day feelings of
joy and sorrow, hope and despair, which are our
normal experiences. If the purpose of art were to
'express' such feelings, to embody them in realistic
pictures, in music or in drama, then art would be
identical with life: a transcript, a report, a reflection.
If the artist did no more than this he might be a good
journalist or a good photographer, but he would not
be venerated as we venerate Michelangelo or

Rembrandt. The purpose of the artist is not to represent emotion, but to transcend it. There are two aphorisms of Georges Braque which describe the true function of emotion in art: 'Emotion is neither added nor imitated: it is the seed, and art is the blossom.' 'I love the rule that corrects emotion; I love the emotion that corrects the rule.' Art is a dialectical process: the resolution of contradictions and ambiguities. A work of art is removed from mundane strife: it is an object of distinterested contemplation. 'Distance', said Simone Weil, 'is the soul of the beautiful: Beauty a fruit which we look at without trying to seize it.' Abstract art is perhaps more distant than any art of the past; it is perhaps also more beautiful.

# AT THE TURN OF A CIVILIZATION

TRADITION is one of those ideological concepts which are used with very different meanings and very different intentions by different people. Mr T. S. Eliot, quite at the beginning of his critical activity, tried to rehabilitate the concept by what is virtually an extension of the accepted meaning. For a static interpretation he substituted a dynamic one. I would not like to suggest that Mr. Eliot, even in 1920, had succumbed to the influence of Bergson, but the tradition of literature is seen as a changing order, a flux, an organism continuously modified by the introduction of new elements. 'The existing order is complete before the new work arrives; for order to persist after the supervention of novelty, the *whole* existing order must be, if ever so slightly, altered; and so the relations, proportions, values of each work of art toward the whole are readjusted; and this is conformity between the old and the new.'*

I was very impressed by this metaphor at the time of its first publication, but had some difficulty in reconciling it with my revolutionary zeal. A little earlier I had been equally impressed by T. E. Hulme's insistence on the *objective* character of

* T. S. Eliot: *The Sacred Wood* (Methuen), 1920, pp. 44-5.

ethical values, and on the necessity for an order or hierarchy among such values that is *absolute*. But Hulme, too, had been a Bergsonian, and his view that art was essentially a breaking through conventional vision and conventional thought – a re-moulding of perception – this again seemed difficult to reconcile with an hierarchy of absolute values.

Philosophizing about the arts in the 1920's was a hazardous occupation because the arts were changing rapidly beneath our eyes. It might be possible to reconcile cubism with tradition – had not Cézanne, from whose practice it was to a large extent derived, declared that his purpose was to continue the tradition of Poussin? But the modern movement in the visual arts did not halt at cubism: from post-impressionism it developed by inevitable stages to expressionism and surrealism, and for the past thirty-five years it has moved rapidly and irrevocably away from any possible concept of tradition. It is no longer a question of modifying an existing order 'ever so slightly': at the present extremes of the modern movement there is not the slightest trace of a pre-existing order; and even the material or technical formulas for the arts of painting and sculpture have been abandoned – the typical modern artist prefers to speak about his constructions or compositions rather than his paintings or carvings. Tradition, which always had some obvious relevance to the *craft* of an art like painting, was abandoned even in this sense: the modern artist has nothing to learn: he 'envelops' his psyche in any material that comes to hand – rubbish, waste-paper, plaster, metal sheets or wires – anything will serve his purpose. We do not sufficiently realize that the traditional concept of the artist himself has been abandoned. In a sense more literal than was perhaps intended by Sri Aurobindo who invented the phrase, or by Coomaraswamy who gave it general currency, *every* man is a particular kind of artist.

It may be said that this is sheer nihilism – formlessness itself has become the aim of art (Nietzsche defined nihilism as 'aimlessness in itself'). But at the same time there has been a corresponding development in psychology and aesthetics which claims significance for the formless, the *gestaltlos*. The absolute distinction between beauty and ugliness, on which traditional aesthetics rested, has disappeared. We now realize 'that the two polar feelings of beauty and ugliness are not so far apart as they may appear to be; to repress unconscious symbolism is the dynamic function of them both.'*

Art, it has often been argued in the past, receives its force and significance from its unconscious symbolism: art has been defined (by Susanne Langer) as the creation of forms *symbolic* of human feeling. But now we have the phenomenon of art anti-art, the nihilistic motive of the Dadaists, art as the destruction of forms that might symbolize human feeling.

* Anton Ehrenzweig: *The Psycho-analysis of Artistic Vision and Hearing*, London (Routledge & Kegan Paul), 1953, p. 80.

How can such art have any relation to tradition? Is tradition a meaningless concept in modern art?

Before we can answer this question we must return to the concept itself and try to define it a little more precisely. In the arts it has become essentially an intellectual concept, but it was not always so. We speak of craft traditions and of stylistic traditions, and in both cases we mean something that can be defined in practical terms. In the Middle Ages the craft of painting, for example, was controlled by a guild (usually dedicated to Saint Luke, who was the patron saint of painters). The guilds may be regarded as the guardians of tradition: their regulations determined the kind of work a painter could accept, the nature and quality of the materials he could use, the organization of his workshop and his relations with his patrons.* Every detail of the process of painting was laid down by the guild regulations, with the result that a code of technical instructions and a standard of technical achievement was maintained unchanged for centuries. If one adds to this the conditions as to subject-matter and treatment laid down by the patron (usually the Church) which extended to every detail of comportment and costume, one can appreciate how confined was the framework within which the medieval artist was allowed to exercise his imagination. That he never-

* For an excellent account of craft traditions in the art of painting see W. G. Constable: *The Painters Workshop* (Oxford University Press), 1954.

theless managed to express so much personal idio-
syncrasy and poetic fantasy is one of the paradoxes of
our subject: a tradition does not necessarily imply
frustration: it is compatible with some kind of
freedom, though the kind has yet to be defined.

Craft traditions remained strong and efficient
until the middle of the eighteenth century – Reynolds's *Discourses* are the final and a most intelligent
formulation of them. They were disrupted, not so
much by the growing spirit of romanticism (for
romanticism is as much in need of craft as any other
ideology) but by economic and social changes. The
social status of the artist had been rising ever since
the fifteenth century, and he gradually divorced
himself from craftsmen like goldsmiths and carpen-
ters and assumed an independent position in society
comparable to that of the scholar. Painting and
sculpture became 'liberal' arts or 'fine' arts as distinct
from applied arts or crafts, and with this change in
status came a loosening of the control exercised by
the guilds. Patronage, too, was changing and instead
of the universal church with its precise requirements,
the painter had to satisfy a multitude of private
patrons each with his individual whim. By the end
of the eighteenth century the guilds had ceased to
control either the quality of paintings or the workshop practice of the painter, but the patron was still
a dictator and would choose, not only subjects after
his own fancy, but even the treatment he desired.
Yet, as Professor Constable has pointed out, 'the

practice of painting for specific places and specific purposes continued until much later than is often supposed, and persisted throughout the nineteenth century. But at the same time, the painter had an increasingly large share in the selection of subject, and became increasingly the final authority as to how it should be treated. Particularly was this the case with easel paintings, whose subjects were chosen without reference to any particular patron or purpose, the painter taking his chance of finding a buyer.'*

As the guilds declined, however, there arose a new guardian of tradition, the Academy. The first academies were already established in Italy in the sixteenth century and by the eighteenth century they had spread throughout Europe and become as tyrannical and as jealous of tradition as ever the guilds had been. Not only did they succeed in confining state and court patronage to their members, but the prestige their members enjoyed meant that private patrons who could afford their services did so – it was a guarantee of quality. Technical standards similar to those of the guilds were enforced in the schools they established, and so the craft tradition was maintained without a break right down to the beginning of the modern period. In this sense Delacroix and Constable, Turner and Cézanne, are still traditional painters. Even painters like Gauguin, Van Gogh and Rousseau, though their work is the foundation of all that is anti-academic in contemporary

* *Op. cit.*, p. 13.

painting, nevertheless were very conscious of 'the existing order' and deliberately strove to emulate it.

It may be a little artificial to try and separate stylistic tradition from craft tradition, but the difference is perhaps obvious. Craft tradition is based on materials and their use, and on the right treatment of specific subjects – on workshop (and later academic) *practice*. Style is an intangible element and is communicated by personal example. Professor Meyer Schapiro has defined it as 'the constant form – and sometimes the constant elements, qualities and expressions – in the art of an individual or a group'* and he proceeds to show how intangible it is as an historical phenomenon. Perhaps one should admit that style and tradition are antithetical terms, for style is basically, in Mr Eliot's sense of the term, individual talent. It spreads from one individual to another, it is contagious, and in that sense we can speak of a constant element in style. If it spreads far enough and deep enough, as did Michelangelo's, then one can give a generic or historical term to the style, such as Mannerism. I do not for a moment question the reality of the concept of style (on the contrary, as will be seen, I regard it as the basic concept in the arts). But a stylistic analysis such as that proposed by Heinrich Wölfflin employs categories – linear as opposed to painterly, closed as opposed to open

* Meyer Schapiro, 'Style', *Anthropology Today* (ed. A. L. Kroeber), University of Chicago Press, 1953, pp. 287.312.

form, the composite as opposed to the fused – all of which are *ex post facto* generalizations, and unless we are to suppose that a tradition can be unconscious (which would seem to be contradictory), such categories are not properly speaking traditional. Indeed, when a style such as Mannerism develops by contagion, it can be said to be anti-traditional – it is a revolt against the prevailing classical tradition. Impressionism is a style in this sense, and it is a revolt against the prevailing academic tradition (a degenerate classical tradition). Other historical analyses of style, such as those of Paul Frankl,* would seem also to be generalizations from phenomena that were originally individualistic and disparate. Style remains, as Goethe defined it, 'an intuition of the inner essence of things' – or as Riegl defined it, 'an active creative process in which new forms arise from the artist's will to solve specifically artistic problems'.† He may be helped to his solution by the knowledge of tools and materials derived from tradition, but the way in which he then solves his problems is peculiar to the artist, and this solution is his style. It is perhaps too late to attempt to confine the concept of 'style' to what is personal or idiosyncratic in a work of art, but I do not find a generalization like 'the Gothic style' very useful: I would prefer to speak of the Gothic *tradition*

* Paul Frankl: *Das System der Kunstwissenschaft*, Brunn and Leipzig (R. M. Rohrer), 1938. Cited by Schapiro.
† Cf. Schapiro, *loc. cit.*, p. 302.

(technique, material and function) and of the style of Giotto (or of the school of Giotto).

These distinctions are perhaps not very important for our present discussion, but it is easy to slip from an expression like the Gothic style to a much more imprecise expression like the Christian style in art. There is no such thing. There is doubtless a Christian tradition in art as in all aspects of the *vita activa*, and this tradition prescribes the form of the basilica, the design of church furniture, the way in which particular saints should be represented and the appropriate symbols for particular feelings. But the style in which the artist or workshop carries out these traditional commissions is the style of the artist himself. Even if we have a more generalized conception of style, the correspondence between style and religious content, as Meyer Schapiro admits, is not at all obvious. 'If the difference between pagan and Christian art is explained broadly by the difference in religious content, there is nevertheless a long period of time – in fact, many centuries – during which Christian subjects are represented in the style of pagan art. As late as A.D. 800, the 'Libri Carolini' speak of the difficulty of distinguishing images of Mary and Venus without the labels.'* Such historical facts are decisive.

With these general considerations in mind, let us approach the contemporary scene. It is one in which

* *Loc. cit.*, p. 305.

273

tradition, in the sense in which we have defined it, does not exist in the arts. It was destroyed in a series of revolts to which we give the names Futurism, Dadaism, Surrealism, Expressionism, etc., and which are all aspects of aesthetic nihilism. Only the ego and his own count in modern art, and though we may use phrases like the Paris School or the New York School, these are merely convenient indications of centres where artists congregate and perhaps influence one another stylistically. There have been attempts to establish a modern tradition – the Bauhaus in Germany is the most conspicuous example, and it failed. Only in architecture a negative tradition of functionalism (i.e. a tradition founded on craft or technique and not on spiritual values) has had some resemblance to the artistic traditions of the past. We sometimes speak of an 'international style' in modern architecture; it is misleading. There is no style in modern architecture because there is nothing specifically artistic in the problems the architect tries to solve. The problems he tries to solve are technical. There is merely a prevailing conformity to technical standards – no problems of *form*, but only of building. As Mies van der Rohe has proclaimed: 'Essentially our task is to free the practice of building from the control of esthetic speculators and restore it to what it should exclusively be: building.'* Aesthetic

* Philip C. Johnson: *Mies van der Rohe*. New York (Museum of Modern Art), 1947, p. 184.

speculators – such as the architects of Hagia Sophia and Chartres!

What happens when a modern architect ignores the advice of Mies van der Rohe and speculates aesthetically? The answer may be found in the church built by Le Corbusier at Ronchamps in France. This church conforms in certain respects to the Christian tradition in architecture: there is a nave with altar, side chapels, stained glass windows, pulpit, porches – that is to say, it functions as a church. But for the rest, although it makes use of modern materials and modern methods of construction, it is a highly speculative exercise in aesthetic values. It has style – the style of the artist, Le Corbusier. I have no means of knowing how effectively it serves its purpose – only the priest and the congregation could tell us that, but when I visited it, it was crowded with devout pilgrims, who seemed to accept its religious atmosphere without question. No conflict, therefore, between this example of contemporary art and the Christian faith.

What of the other visual arts, more particularly the arts of painting and sculpture? Here the evidence is much more difficult to collect and assess. We have in England a church in the city of Northampton for which a statue of the Madonna and Child and a painting of the Crucifixion were commissioned some years ago. The statue is by Henry Moore, the painting by Graham Sutherland. The church itself is a pleasing example of the Neo-gothic 'style' (there is some justification for using the word style in this context, because the church is an individual architect's interpretation of the Gothic tradition in architecture), and these two contemporary works look perfectly dignified and appropriately decorative in their setting. But they are not, of course, Gothic or Neo-gothic in 'style': each is an expression of the artist's individuality. Both artists have accepted a traditional theme, but interpreted it in an un-traditional manner.

It may be that when our descendants get far enough away from it, the riotous individualism of our contemporary art will have the appearance of another epoch of Mannerism. Time has the effect of giving unity to what appears at the moment to be a multiplicity. But if at some future date the works of Picasso, Klee, Max Ernst, Kandinsky, Miró, Mondrian, Léger, Sutherland, Pollock, and hundreds more focus into some stylistic unity, a unity of style it will be and not one of tradition. Tradition demands what the modern artist rejects: discipline, conformity, humility. It may be an inherent tendency for the Christian to seek the security and the self-effacing service of an artistic tradition. But he cannot have it in our age, or in any easily conceivable future. It is not for me to speculate about the future of the Christian faith; I do not regard that future as necessarily incompatible with the irremediable individualism of modern art.

We have in England a beautiful and humble Christian artist (a poet as well as a painter) whose name is David Jones. He has written with far more understanding of these problems than I, for he is not only a good artist but a devout Christian. I would like to conclude with the fragment of a poem which he wrote and abandoned about 1938 – it seems to express the essential truth about the problem to which this volume is devoted:

I said, ah! what shall I write?
I inquired up and down
        (he's tricked before
with his manifold lurking places).
I looked for his symbol at the door.
I have looked for a long while
        at the textures and contours
I have run a hand over trivial intersections.
I have journeyed among the dead forms causation
projects from pillar to pylon. I have tired the
eyes of the mind regarding the colours and lights.
I felt for his wounds
        in nozzles and containers.
I have wondered for the automatic devices . . . I
have tested the inane patterns without prejudice.
I have been on my guard to not condemn the
    unfamiliar
. . . for it is easy to miss him at the turn of a
civilization . . .*

* David Jones: *Epoch and Artist*. Selected writings edited by Harman Grisewood. London (Faber), 1959, p. 179.

# NOTE

*Of the writings included in this volume, the 'Letter to a Young Painter' is here printed for the first time. 'The Ambiguous Critic' was published in a French translation in L'Œil (December 1960). 'The Artist's Dilemma' was broadcast in German by the University of the Air, Berlin, in July 1961. 'The Ambiguity of Modern Sculpture' was delivered as an address to the Royal Swedish Academy of Fine Arts on the occasion of the Sergel Festival, February 26th, 1960. 'The Social Significance of Abstract Art' was a contribution to the Europa-Gespräch, a conference held in Vienna in June 1960; it was subsequently published in Quadrum (No. 9). 'Why Abstract?' was written for the New York Times Magazine and appeared in the issue of April 17th, 1960. 'At the Turn of a Civilization' was written for a symposium on Christian Faith and the Contemporary Arts published by the Abingdon Press, New York, 1962. The shorter essays on individual artists were written on the occasion of the various exhibitions of their work held during the past fifteen years. The essay on Henry Moore is a consolidation of three or four such notices, the second part being an address (delivered in absentia) at the opening of an exhibition in Berlin in July 1961.*